In Understan[ding] ... transparently sha[res ...] journey. From humble beginnings in China du[ring] historical events of the '80s and '90s to a season of deep, lonely struggles in Japan and then on to the glamour and prestige of becoming a Goldman Sachs wealth advisor and business owner, he has much to teach us about what truly matters. The book will touch your heart and open your eyes to a more excellent way.
**Chuck Bentley; CEO, Crown Financial Ministries;
Founder, Christian Economic Forum**

Lu's story proves once again that grandparents who give love, encourage good habits and thoughtful questions of their grandchildren will leave a legacy for generations to come. Get ready for a great read!
Brad Formsma – best-selling author of I Like Giving and host of the WOW factor podcast

Lu Dong's remarkable journey, from a hungry student in Tokyo to a Wall Street banker and from being an entrepreneur to a deeper spiritual calling, is a testament to the extraordinary tapestry woven by God's providence. His story of growth, survival and faith invites us to reflect on the amazing journey of life and the role of faith within it. An inspiring read that beautifully illustrates how God's grace and love unfold in unexpected ways.
Carl Thong; Chairman of Sunstone Group

Lu Dong has lived several lifetimes in his still-emerging story. He writes beautifully and honestly about his geographic journey from China to the USA and Japan, about his career journey from Goldman Sachs to Stanford GSB to three-time entrepreneur and most importantly, about his journey of finding purpose and peace in the idols of status, financial security and success in the business world to finding it in the Creator God of the Universe. Looking forward to reading "Season 2"!

John Watkins – Co-Principal, COhatch Regional Development Ventures, LLC. John was twice elected chairman of The American Chamber of Commerce in China and was active in US-China commercial relations for three decades.

UNDERSTANDING THE WAY

懂路

A journey from personal survival and success to servant leadership

Copyright © 2023 Lu Dong

The moral right of the author has been asserted.

Apart from any fair dealing for the purposes of research or private study, or criticism or review, as permitted under Copyright, Design and Patents Act 1998, this publication may only be reproduced, stored or transmitted, in any form or by any means, with prior permission in writing of the publishers, or in any case of the reprographic reproduction in accordance with the terms of licences issued by the Copyright Licensing Agency. Enquiries concerning reproduction outside these terms should be sent to the publishers.

PublishU Ltd

www.PublishU.com

Scripture taken from the Holy Bible, New King James Version,
© 1982 by Thomas Nelson, Inc.
All rights reserved.

Scripture from the Holy Bible, New International Version®, NIV®.
Copyright © 1973, 1978, 1984, 2011 by Biblica, Inc.™ Used by permission of Zondervan. All rights reserved worldwide.

Scripture taken from the Holy Bible, New Living Translation,
copyright ©1996, 2004, 2007
by Tyndale House Foundation. Used by permission of Tyndale House Publishers, Inc.,
Carol Stream, IL 60188. All rights reserved.

All rights of this publication are reserved.

Thanks

I'd like to thank my grandfather Dong E, who I wrote a lot about in this book. He is one of the few humans I admire the most and impacted my life.

I'd like to thank my grandmother Li Ling. I didn't mention her much in this book; however, she is a role model of our family values which influenced me from childhood.

I'd like to thank my father Dong Jin Sheng and my mother Zhang Wan Rong for raising me and teaching me the basic values for my life.

I'd like to thank my wife Hideko for going through the ups and downs together. She is always positive and calm. She gives me complete freedom to take risks. She is like an anchor to me.

I'd like to thank my best friends and colleagues, Ory Li and Akira Saito. Thank you for walking the journey with me. You have always been sober and helpful so that I can always know who I am.

I'd like to thank Ikemoto-san for helping me understand "Nattoku" and honesty. Always seek understanding and consent from people instead of pushing my ideas through.

I'd like to thank my Christian brother, Carl Thong, who mentored me to apply biblical principles to my business. Carl introduced me to the Faith Driven Entrepreneur and Christian Economic Forum. I met leaders such as Henry Kaestner and Chuck Bentley who successfully built those organisations to showcase, share and foster Christians to make a difference in the marketplace and use their businesses to worship God and help human flourishing.

Finally, I'd like to thank Matt Bird for coaching me to write my first book in three months.

Content

Foreword

Chapter 1 Values Learned From my Grandfather

Chapter 2 Values Learned From my Father

Chapter 3 Dreams Came True in High School

Chapter 4 Gave Up Dreams, Went for the Money

Chapter 5 Way to Japan, Survival Game

Chapter 6 Blossom In Saitama University

Chapter 7 Learnings and Struggles at Goldman Sachs

Chapter 8 Road to Stanford

Chapter 9 Transformational Experiences at Stanford

Chapter 10 Joined a VC Firm in China

Chapter 11 Start my First Company in China, Beyond Tailors: Shirts of Dell

Chapter 12 Start my Second Company in China: La Miu, the Victoria's Secret of China

Chapter 13 Start my Third Company in Japan: TakeMe, Copy From China

About the Author

LU DONG

Foreword

My name in Chinese, 董路, means 'understanding the way'. Some used to joke that I should be a tour guide.

I journeyed my life from dreaming in China to surviving in Tokyo... washing dishes in Tokyo to Goldman Sachs in New York City... doing exams at Saitama University to writing papers at Stanford University... a consultant at Monitor to a venture capitalist at GGV Capital... from marketing lingerie in China to selling foodtech in Japan...

My life so far has been full of unexpected turns and ups and downs. I work hard. I have always been busy.

Covid gave me a great chance to pause and reflect on my life at fifty.

I began understanding my true identity, values and motivation.

It's still a journey halfway. I feel I still have a long way to go. However, it's a journey of enlightenment.

Now, I am ready to be a tour guide in life.

I hope by sharing the stories of my life, I can help others to think about those ultimate questions about their lives:

"Who am I?"

"Why do I do what I am doing every day?"

"What am I going to achieve using my time and talents?"

I hope everyone can have a unique and fulfilling journey in their lives.

LU DONG

Chapter 1
Values Learned From my Grandfather

My name, Dong Lu, in Chinese means understanding the way. Dong means understanding, Lu means road or way. I heard my father gave this name to me, hoping I could understand the meaning of life and walk the right way. After fifty years, I still feel I barely understand the meaning of life and it's still hard to walk the right way.

The environment when I grew up

I spent a lot of time during my childhood with my grandfather, Dong E. Our three generations of the family lived together in a small two-bedroom apartment in Beijing until we moved out when I was ten. My grandfather used to be a professor at Tsing Hua University. My father and his two sisters were all born and raised on campus. Tsing Hua University is vast. It's like a small city with about two hundred thousand students and faculty living on campus. There are supermarkets, hospitals, elementary schools and high schools.

When the Beijing Institute of Iron and Steel Engineering was founded, my grandfather moved there with the whole family and started teaching metallurgy. I was born on the campus as well. That area was in the Northwest corner of Beijing; it had eight universities, including the famous Beijing University. The address was University

Avenue. The Summer Palace was only thirty minutes away by bicycle. The area was full of culture and history. There were lots of farmland outside the campus. Those rice fields were my favourite playground when I was a boy. We used to fish for frogs in the summer when there was plenty of water in the field. In the fall, after harvesting, we used to catch grasshoppers, put them on a stick, fry them and eat them.

Like many parents in China, they left their children to their grandparents because they had to work. I enjoyed spending time with my grandparents. I started going to elementary school at seven until we moved out when I was ten.

My memories of my grandfather were full of love, happiness and fun! He was kind and gentle, always smiling at me. He was patient and never got angry no matter how naughty I was. While my dad hit me often, my grandpa never hit me. My grandpa was big and muscular. He was like an elephant when he walked, slow but strong. I used to swim on his back in the lake of the Summer Palace. I felt he was like a whale.

Be curious and dare to ask questions: "There are no stupid questions, only stupid answers"

The game I loved to play the most with him was to ask him ten questions a day. He bought me this series of books called One Hundred Thousand Questions. I remember when I asked him why the sun came up from the east and went down in the west, he was so excited and told everyone in the family: Lu was a genius to ask such a great question. There were days I ran out of questions. My grandpa always encouraged me to ask about anything: "There are no stupid questions, only stupid answers."

Be honest about things you don't know. If there is anything you don't know, look it up now, don't wait

I remember there were times he was honest and said to me, I don't know the answers, let's find out together. Then he looked up answers from dictionaries or books and showed me the answer. Whenever I asked him a question, he answered me immediately. When he needed to look up books, he did it immediately even in the middle of a meal. My grandma sometimes complained to him, "Can you guys do it after the meal? The food is getting cold!" He would answer: "No, I will forget then. I need to do it now!" He was excited when he found the answer. Then I jumped on his lap and listened to his explanation.

You are your habit. Form the right habit. Get rid of bad habits at an early stage

My grandfather always told me to form the right habits. He always told me to wash my dishes right after the meal, always throw the apple core in the trash bin right after eating an apple and not put it on the table. He said: "Would you not wipe your butt after a dump and wipe it after three days? No, you do it right away! Wiping your butt is part of the dump. Washing dishes is part of the

meal; until you wash your dishes, your meal is not over."
"You may feel painful to wash dishes. You may feel comfortable and be lazy by putting the dishes in the sink for now, but you must wash them anyway in the future. The pain will not go away, it will be accumulated over time and you will have to face more pain in the future. If you wash them now for a few more minutes, you can feel good about the completion of the meal and lay back and watch TV and never worry about washing dishes until the next meal. How much more can you enjoy the TV? Furthermore, if you habitually wash dishes right after the meal, you won't feel the pain anymore. It becomes part of the routine. So which one do you choose?"

Never force me to do anything, always speak reason and argue logically (讲道理)

My grandfather always kindly persuaded me about his ideas with reasons and logic. He never forced me to do anything by his power. He always showed me how to do it himself and offered to do it together. He always gave me choices and respected my choices. When I made my choice, he always said, "See, I know Lu is a good boy who is reasonable and think logically." I felt that in my grandfather's mind, being reasonable was the foundation for mutual respect and treating others.

Treat everyone equally and be kind to everyone

My grandpa liked to ask questions as well. When we went out for a walk in the fields or on the street, he always had small talks with the farmers and workers. I didn't understand what they were talking about, but they seemed to have a good time. He always had great conversations with anyone he met, no matter who they were. He treated everyone equally and had a genuine interest in others.

Learn not only from books but from nature

My grandpa was not a typical professor who always wore a pair of glasses and a white lab coat and taught in a classroom. He loved the outdoors. He was good at Tai chi. He always performed Tai chi in the playground, while my friends and I were copying him. I felt his personality was like Tai chi, slow but firm, soft but strong, calm and everlasting.

His favourite activity was to take us to natural parks and rivers at the weekends. I was among the first of my friends to get a bicycle, which was a luxury item back then. Everyone in our family had a bicycle. On the weekend, we would form a bicycle team of five or six bicycles to go out to parks such as Yuan Ming Yuan, the Summer Palace, or the canals outside Summer Palace. In the summer, we swam, fished and had picnics. My grandpa and my dad used to make fish nets by themselves. They threw nets into the river to catch fish. It was always a lot of joy to watch them pull the nets from the river and discover what was in them. Sometimes there were lots of small fish. Sometimes there were shells, clams, boots and bottles. No matter what came up we were happy. For picnics, we had bread with dry fruits, sausages, eggs and fruits. Summer is my favourite season because I was born in the summer. However, winter was long in Beijing, we always went ice skating in rivers and lakes. I didn't have my own ice-skating shoes. I had to wear my father's shoes by putting a lot of paper inside the shoes and tying the laces very tight. My grandma told me that's how my dad learned to skate by wearing my grandpa's ice-skating shoes. I remember I became very good and skated through the legs of adults. There were many holes in the ice of the lake for the fish to breathe. I fell into the holes a couple of times. I remember I fell into an ice hole in the back lake of Summer Palace. It was so cold that when I had to hang my pants to dry, the pants became frozen and rigid like a rock. My family covered me with their clothes. I wore plastic bags on my feet and bicycled home.

The springs and falls in Beijing were beautiful as well. The red leaves of Beijing in Xiang Mountain were famous. We used to play games to call the names of plants, flowers and insects when we went out in the mountains and parks.

Don't tell me; show me. Do it with me; let's do it together

One of my grandpa's favourite activities was photography. He brought back a Russian camera from his scholarship at Moscow University. Cameras back then were considered luxury items as they cost years of income for an average family in China. My grandpa allowed me to use his camera and taught me how to use a rangefinder camera to focus by turning the ring on the lens, so the two shades became one in the middle part of the viewfinder. He told me the rules of exposure by changing the shutter speed and aperture. After a day of outdoor activity and photo shooting, we came home and developed films by ourselves. We turned the toilet into a darkroom by covering the windows and changing the light bulb to red. We spent hours and hours in the darkroom developing films. It was magical to see the pictures gradually appear in the solution. Then we dried them up and cut them into different sizes.

Later when I went to elementary school, my grandpa bought me a small plastic camera from Russia, it took half-frame pictures and had no focus mechanism. I had to guess the distance between the camera and the subject. I became the official cameraman on school outings. I took pictures of the whole class, developed the films in our toilet darkroom for everyone in the class and gave them out afterwards. I used that camera until high school.

My grandpa always encouraged me to do whatever I wanted to do. When he found I loved drawing, he put me in drawing classes, from sketching to Chinese painting. He bought many books for me to learn from. I won many awards in the district. Many of my drawings were hanging in my high school when I visited ten years ago.

When I later got into a university in Japan and talked with my peer students about my youth, they were always amazed by my stories. They always said it was like listening to their grandparents' stories. For example, we had our first nine-inch black and white TV when I was seven. We then changed to a twelve-inch black and white TV two years later. We didn't have refrigerators and washing machines. We only bought enough food for a couple of days of usage. We used to hang meat or fish out of the window in the winter. Sometimes cats came and ate some of it. We washed clothes by hand on a washing board with soap. In the winter, the clothes became frozen and hard like rocks. There was no hot water or shower in our home. We had to go to the public bath once a week. After taking a bath in the winter, my hair froze on the way home.

Except for food, we never went shopping. We made everything by ourselves, such as clothes and furniture. My grandmother, mother and aunts in the family made clothes for everyone. I learned how to sew using needles and threads. Later, I learned how to use a sewing machine and embroidery. My grandfather and father made all the furniture, such as tables, chairs, sofas and closets by themselves. I used to watch my grandfather and father use all kinds of tools to work with wood to make furniture. They also used different kinds of colours and paint to paint the furniture layer after layer. I had a younger sister. She was two and a half years younger than me. She went to a kindergarten and only came home on the weekends. I learned to make a robot and a cart from wood for her. I gave them to her as presents when we picked her up at the bus stop.

That was the family environment in my childhood. We didn't have much money. We had a simple and happy life. I learned that whatever we wanted, we made them by ourselves.

Do the right thing. Have a clearcut stand on what to love and what to hate

My grandfather was always patient and always talked gently with a smile. He seldom got angry. There were only two times I remember he got angry.

Once was when he got to know that my father hit me after seeing the bruises around my body. He told my father: "You can't treat a little boy with violence like that! He is a good boy who understands the reasons. You should always convince him with reasons instead of beating him. Beating doesn't solve problems. It will create more problems."

However, my father didn't seem to listen to him. I remember they quarrelled many times over my education. My father always complained that my grandfather spoiled me. I remember they were both very upset and went into silence after the quarrel. I felt our moving out had something to do with their disagreement.

The other time my grandfather got angry was after the Tiananmen Massacre. He was furious: "They shouldn't fire guns at the students. It's not right! This is not reasonable. Why not talk about reasons and argue with logic? The students would have listened! Nobody will tell the truth if they just kill people like that!" "When I was young, I was a student fighting for freedom and democracy in China. Kuomintang fired guns at us. They thought they could suppress righteousness by killing us. However, we defeated them. Today, I can't believe the Chinese Communist Party is doing the same! This is not the party I joined." He wrote letters to China's top leaders, Deng Xiaoping and Jiang Zemin and he resigned as a

CCP member. Although he never got replies directly from the leaders, many people came to persuade my grandfather not to resign from the party.

My grandfather gathered us for a family meeting after he sent letters to the leaders of the CCP. He told us he sacrificed his family, broke up with his rich father and joined the revolution. He joined the Chinese Communist Party and organised student movements to fight with Kuomintang because he believed the old China should be turned upside down for the freedom and equality of the poor. He chased the dream of communism and devoted his entire life to it. He survived the suppression and persecution by Kuomintang and persevered for twenty-eight years until Kuomintang was defeated. It was bliss when the New China was established. He felt his dream came true and everyone was fanatical about realising communism for the whole world. However, soon he was labeled the Rightest and sent to the farm where he lived with cows. He endured it. During the ten years of the Cultural Revolution, everything was taken away, his family was divided. He endured and hoped China would be better again after the chaos. He believed it was a growing pain. CCP was trying to figure out the right way. After all, they had never run a country with the largest population on earth before. However, this time, it's different. The government fired guns at the students who were trying to tell the truth. Their intention was to make China better. He taught his students all these years that his role was not just to teach them knowledge and be smarter, but to teach them about the truth and how to be a human. He used this word again, "Reasonable (讲道理)". He said: "The government should talk to the students with reasons and argue logically. Killing and violence never lead to righteousness and never will defeat righteousness." He had lost hope for the party and the government completely. He painfully and sadly told us: "Honest people will not have a good future in this country anymore. I am old. I am done. You should leave the country and have a better future somewhere else."

Love: a continuous effort to think about others and try to make others' lives better

My grandpa had the most Impact on me as a role model in my life. He is the person I respect the most in my life. I am sure I am not the only one. I could feel he loved me and cared about me very much. I was his first and only grandson.

When I went to Japan in 1993, he started writing one letter every month to me. I had no friends in Japan in the first year when I got to Japan. Every day, my hope was to check the mailbox to see if there were any letters from China. Once every month, guaranteed, there was a letter from my grandfather. In the letters, not only did he encourage me to go to college and work in Japan, but also, he encouraged me to go to MBA in the US. He attached some news clippings of MBA rankings in the world. He told me how smart I was and at least I should get a master's degree in the US.

Eighty-four Letters and the funeral

In February 2000, my grandfather died of a sudden heart attack on Chinese New Year's Eve. One night, I got a call from my grandmother while eating in a ramen restaurant in Tokyo. I was shocked and didn't know how to process it. Tears were blurring my sight when I was riding my motorcycle home. I got home; there was a letter, half written, sitting on my desk. It was a letter to my grandfather that I had been writing for a couple of weeks.

I was working at Goldman Sachs in Tokyo. I had a busy life, working one hundred hours a week. I had enough money so I could make an international phone call to my grandparents occasionally. However, my grandfather always asked me to write letters to him, because he could read my letters repeatedly. Looking at this unfinished letter, I cried even harder. I blamed myself, too lazy and had too many excuses for not writing letters to my grandfather earlier.

I started to collect the letters that my grandfather wrote to me. I counted, there were eighty-four letters. I came to Japan in May 1993 and until January 2000, there were exactly eighty-four months! I started to read every letter. I could tell his handwriting started to get more and more cursive. That showed his healthy condition had gradually got worse and worse.

I decided to finish the letter I wrote to my grandfather and bring it to the funeral. I wrote and wrote, pouring all my memories about him and how much I love him, miss him and respect him. I wrote fourteen pages until the morning. I felt I had a good conversation with him.

I immediately flew back to Beijing for the funeral. My father and my grandmother were trying to send a notification to my grandfather's friends and former colleagues to attend the funeral by collecting contacts and through archived letters. They were only able to find about one hundred and fifty names.

On the funeral day, surprisingly, there were about five hundred people who showed up. The age of the people who came to the funeral ranged from their twenties to their nineties. They were from my grandfather's students to his elementary school teacher who was over ninety years old. He came in a wheelchair. Some flew for four hours all the way from Guangdong. I guess they got the information by word of mouth.

Standing by my grandfather's body, watching people passing by to have the last look at my grandfather's body, I was amazed. What did my grandfather do to their lives so that they came from far away to see a cold body? My grandfather couldn't do anything for them anymore. Then this scene came to my mind. It was the scene described in the book, The Seven Habits of Highly Effective People by Stephen Covey. In chapter 2, Begin with the End in Mind, Stephen had the readers imagine their own funeral. Who would come? What would they say about you?

After the funeral, our family came back to our grandparents' home and talked about our grandfather. We were all amazed by how many people came to the funeral. I started sharing my story of the eighty-four letters my grandfather wrote to me. Suddenly, one of my aunts who lived far away from Beijing said: "I get a letter every month from my father too!" And one of my cousins said: "I get a letter from my grandfather every month too!" Then we all realised our grandfather wrote a letter to all of us who lived far away every month! There was a vision in front of me: my grandfather was sitting in front of his desk, writing letters for each of us. He paused from time to time to think about what we needed, clipped newspapers and attached to the letters. Wow! What an amazing love he had for all of us! Furthermore, if he did this to our family members, he could do this to his students, his friends, his teachers... He always thought about others and cared about others for their best interests.

I looked around his apartment, the most expensive thing he had left was a thirty-two-inch colour TV which was bought by my father. However, looking at the people in the room and thinking about the people who came to the funeral, I realised that they were the legacy of my grandfather. I am also part of it! At that moment, I realised my grandfather still lived in the hearts of those people. My grandfather's life made a difference in those people's lives so that they remembered him. No wonder there were so many people who came to see him for the last time. They came to see my grandfather for the last time to pay respect to him. We all felt we were the best when we were with him.

I also thought about my work. I was struggling as a young professional at Goldman Sachs, working hard, trying to gain people's respect. My role models were the young managing directors who made millions of dollars in their thirties. They lived in big apartments, drove Ferraris around and had big house parties with hundreds of beautiful people. I thought about their funerals, how many people would come? There would be no money and no parties for those people. Would they fly from different parts of the world to come and see a cold body? What's their legacy?

I realised the legacy came from how much positive impact one had made in other people's lives, not from money, title, or material things.

Before the cremation, I put my letter in the pocket of my grandfather's jacket. It was cremated with his body. I was sure he would read the letter in heaven because he still lived in my heart. His value continued to guide me to be a person like him.

LU DONG

Chapter 2
Values Learned From My Father

At the age of ten, during my third grade in elementary school, we moved out of our grandparents' house and moved into our own apartment. My memory of childhood about my parents was that they were always busy at work. In the morning, they left together on a shuttle bus to work. My younger sister was seven and went to grade one. We went to the same school together by forming a line with kids living in the same neighbourhood and walking to school. I had a key hanging around my neck. At noon, we came home and cooked for ourselves. Usually, we cooked some simple instant noodles or heated up the leftovers from the previous day. One day my younger sister tried to turn on the gas oven by lighting up a match. As she put her face close to the oven to watch the fire, the gas fired suddenly and the flame burned her eyelashes, eyebrows and some of the hair on her forehead.

After lunch, we went to school again for classes. After school, we played around our apartment and waited for our parents to come home. When the shuttle bus stopped, we rushed to our parents and hugged them. My mum looked at my sister's face and said, "What happened to your eyelashes and eyebrows?" We told them what happened and she held my sister in her arms and cried.

As we grew up a little bit, we were given the responsibility of preparing dinner, since it was too late sometimes when my parents came home after work to go to the markets to buy food and cook. It gets dark by five pm in winter in Beijing. My parents gave us some cash. We went to the markets to buy meat and vegetables for dinner. Sometimes, we washed the vegetables, cut them and waited for our parents to cook when they came home. Later, I could cook some simple dishes, such as stir fry eggs and tomatoes by myself.

It's not about winning the fight; it's about showing them you have the spirit to fight

The change of school had a lot of negative impact on me. First, I didn't have many friends and got bullied by the kids in school and the bigger kids who lived in our neighbourhood. Then I lost interest in going to school. Going to school wasn't an enjoyable experience anymore.

One morning, I was excited to be wearing a brand-new jacket made by my grandmother. On the way to school, a tall boy laughed at me and said, "look at him, a new jacket!" Then he started to wrestle me and put me down in a muddy puddle. My face and body were bruised and bleeding. My new jacket was completely torn and ruined by the dirty water. I stood there watching them walking away and laughing; tears came from my eyes. I was burning with anger. Why?! Why did they do this to me?

I told my parents about this after school. My mother washed and repaired the jacket for me. My father got very angry and took me to the parents of the boy who beat me. They scolded the boy in front of me and had him apologise to me. On the way home, my father told me: "Next time someone tries to beat you, you fight back. Eye for an eye, tooth for a tooth." I replied: "But they are much bigger than me…" My father told me: "It's not about winning the fight; it's about showing them you have the spirit to fight. You will never surrender to them even if they kill you."

My father bought me a new green bicycle with twenty-six-inch wheels as I grew taller, replacing my twenty-inch wheel bicycle. I was very happy. We could go to farther places during the weekends with the new bicycle. I locked it in the hallway of our apartment.

One afternoon, I came back from school and saw many kids playing in front of our apartment building with my bicycle. A tall boy older than us somehow took my bicycle from the hallway, unlocked it and rode on it with other kids. They knocked the bicycle over and over and broke many parts. When they saw me, they did not get off the bicycle and kept riding it and laughing at me. I got angry and tried to get my bicycle back. The tall boy got off the bicycle and started beating me. He was so intimidating and strong; I couldn't fight back. The only thing I could do was cling to his jacket, no matter how much he beat my face, my eyes and my body, I just didn't let go of my hands. Blood came from my eyes; I couldn't see clearly. I fell to the ground but still clung to his jacket. He was cursing and beating and kicking, but no matter how hard he tried, he couldn't get my hands off his jacket. Finally, he was tired and shouted at me: "Get your hands off my jacket, otherwise…" I shouted: "Kill me! Kill me! If you don't kill me today, I am gonna kill you one day!" I didn't know if it was because of my voice or my face that scared them. All the kids, including the tall boy, went silent. They stared at me and didn't say anything. The tall boy shook his head and became powerless. I finally let go of him, stood on my feet and stared at him. It was all red in front of my vision. I felt like I was shooting fire at him. After a period of silence, all the kids started to scatter away.

From then on, I never got bullied in my neighbourhood or in school.

One push-up a day; never give up

I was a small kid in elementary school. In grade three, some girls were even taller than me and they ran faster than me. I was the shortest kid sitting in the classroom's front row. Taller kids sat in the back rows. All the kids grew taller after one year. Some boys shifted to more back rows. However, I always stayed in the front row for the entire elementary school. Furthermore, I was weak. I heard from my parents that I had pneumonia when I was two. It almost killed me. After that, I became very skinny and weak. I didn't eat or sleep much compared to other kids. I couldn't even stand straight.

I was the smallest boy in the class during my first year in junior high school. Sport was never my strength. I never enjoyed PE at school.

One day, there was a test in PE class for boys. Ten push-ups were the passing mark; eighteen push-ups were the full mark. All the boys formed a circle and watched one boy do push-ups in the middle of the circle one at a time.

All the boys watching counted: "One, two, three..." The teacher kept the score. It was my turn. Knowing I was the weakest in the class, some boys shouted at me, "How many can you do?" I felt embarrassed and said: "I can do one hundred!" "One hundred? It's impossible! Let's see how many he can do!" The boys shouted and laughed around me. I got down on the ground and pushed my arms with all my strength. I gritted my teeth and held my breath; I felt my body as heavy as a stone. My arms were shaking; sweat started to drop from my forehead... And finally, I ran out of strength and fell flat to the ground. I couldn't even do one. All the boys were laughing around me. "Hahaha, one hundred! He couldn't even do one!" I was so embarrassed. I didn't get up; I kept my face facing the ground. I wished there was a crack that I could slip in and hide myself. The teacher pulled me up and shook his head. He told the other boys to be quiet. "Next!"

My father was a tall and muscular man. He was one hundred and eighty-three cm tall. In his generation, he was among the tallest in China. He was easy to be spotted in the crowd because he always stood out. He was an athlete in swimming and basketball. I remember I used to play with his biceps. They were hard like rocks and big like mountains. To me, he was too perfect to imitate. He told me he was number two at a student swimming contest in Beijing. He was also handsome. One day, when we got on a bus, there was a lady whispered to me asking if my dad was an actor. He was always confident and right. He was very strict with me in everything in life. He used to go to the army. He taught me how to fold my comforters neatly and square-shaped, just like in the army. He trained me to dress in one minute in the middle of the night without a light. However, when he laughed, he was charming with white and beautifully aligned teeth.

I told my father what happened in PE class. My father asked me: "Do you want to do one push-up?" I said: "Yes.". He said: "OK, let's just try to do one push-up today." My favourite time was after dinner when we walked around the neighbourhood. My father said: "Can you try to do one push-up?" As in the PE class, I couldn't push myself from the ground. "OK, let's make it easier." He found a stair and told me to do push-ups from a raised stair. I used all my strength and barely did one. "Great! You just did your first push-up! We are done today. Tomorrow, we are going to do one push-up again. No need to hurry, just do one push-up a day." The next day, we went for a walk after dinner. I did the same. But I felt a little smoother. My father told me: "See! You are doing better!" I could confidently do one push-up on the stair the next day. I felt good. The next day, my father asked me, "Do you want to try to do two push-ups?" I nodded at him. I took a deep breath and held it. One, two! The second one was shaky, but I did it. "Now you can do two push-ups! That's fast!" My father encouraged me. After a couple of days, doing two push-ups on a stair was easy. Two weeks later, I could do seven push-ups on a stair! My father asked me: "Now, let's try to do one push-up on the ground." I did it! "Just like you can do seven push-ups on a stair, you will do seven on the ground soon. No hurry, one push-up a day!" Day in and day out, doing push-ups with my father after dinner became my routine and it was fun.

One year later, we had to do the same push-up test again in the PE class. This time, eighteen was the passing mark;

thirty-six was the full mark. Boys grew fast. Many kids could pass eighteen, but no one could do thirty-six. It was my turn. I got in the centre of the circle. Many boys were laughing and whispering to each other. "Can he do even one push-up?!" I took a deep breath and told myself, "One push-up a day." All the memories of when I did push-ups with my father during the year flashed back in my mind. One, two, three, four... The boys started to count. eighteen, nineteen, twenty... Their voice got louder and louder. I kept pushing and gritted my teeth. Counting my push-ups, boys around me started to shout and jump. Thirty-four! Thirty-five! Thirty-six!! I used all my power and got up from the ground. I was exhausted. My face was red and sweated all around my face. But I never felt so great! The boys were surprised and excited. They rushed to hug me. The teacher hugged me too. It was a miracle. I was so proud. Although I was still the smallest boy in the class. I raised my head high. I felt I was tall.

It's thirty, not thirty!

I transferred to a junior high school a little over a year ago. During my first junior high school, I studied Russian as a foreign language. Russian was the most widely studied foreign language in my grandfather's and father's generation. My grandfather was fluent in Russian. He was a visiting scholar at Moscow University for many years. My parents went to a military university where everybody studied Russian. However, since my generation, English has become more and more popular. Russian became a niche language. Our family's initial decision was for me to study Russian because we believed I would one day go to Russia for college. However, after one year, we felt that

English would be a permanent trend for our generation. We decided to change schools to a junior high school that studied English. We chose the junior high school of the Beijing Iron and Steel Institute.

Again, I was in a disadvantageous situation. Not only did I not have any friends, but also, I was one year behind everybody in English class. I sat in the English class and understood nothing. The English teacher knew the situation. She never asked me any questions in the class.

At home, my father studied with me every night. He said: "I studied Russian. Now it's a great opportunity that I am going to study English together with you. Let's learn a few words every day." We started to follow an English-teaching radio programme that a Canadian company did. My parents and I were pronouncing loudly after the voice on the radio. Day in and day out, I started to remember more and more words in English. I started to understand more and more in the class. After a couple of months, the English teacher started to see my progress in my homework. She knew I could answer some simple questions. One day, for the first time, she asked me a question in the class. The question was easy; the answer was "thirty". I stood up. Everybody was looking at me since I never spoke a word in the English class. The teacher smiled and nodded with encouragement. I spoke nervously, "Thirty". All the students started to laugh and imitated me. "Thirty! Thirty." I didn't know what went wrong and quickly went through the question in my mind. "Yes, the answer should be thirty." The teacher instructed the students to calm down and said to me with a smile. "Yes, your answer was right, thirty. However, your pronunciation was not correct. It should be thirty (thuhtee,

British English accent), but not thirty (thurtee, American English accent)." Oh, I finally realised that the English taught in school was British English, whereas at home, the English radio we were listening to every day was Canadian English. I started to enjoy English and it became my favourite class.

Be a happy number two

Our school published rankings of students on the wall outside of each classroom. Students and their parents cared about their ranking and scores because only the top students could attend good senior high schools. The students were very competitive. I was among the top ten per cent of the class, with a few subjects ranked number one.

One day, my father looked at my ranking and scores and told me a story. When he was in high school, he loved to do everything. The main subjects such as math, physics and chemistry and the extra curriculum classes, such as singing, musical instruments, swimming, basketball, drawing, etc. He was active in many scenes in school, such as music festivals, sports contests and drawing contests. There was a girl in his class who was always serious and studied hard only in the main subjects. She made number one in all the main subjects. However, she never went to extra curriculum classes. In PE class, she was always sick and didn't perform well.

One year, she got number two in a subject. She became very upset. She studied harder and played less with other kids. However, her scores got worse in the next term.

Before graduation, she got very sick and couldn't continue studying at school. My father and his classmates went to visit her at home. However, she never returned to school. My father told me: "She was never happy, never satisfied with herself. Being number one was her only motivation to study. She could never forgive herself for being number two. Whereas I studied hard enough in the main subjects. At the same time, keep a wide range of interests in other extra curriculums. I enjoyed learning everything and had many friends even until today." "Test scores were just results. If you put in one hundred per cent effort and have no excuse, you don't need to pay too much attention to the scores and ranking themselves. What's more important was what you really learned and enjoyed and had a good balance of ethics, intelligence and physical strength and endurance." My father continued: "I'd rather see you a balanced and happy number two than an unhappy and narrow-minded number one."

I followed my father's guidance. I followed my passion and tried almost everything I could do. I enjoyed my school years and had many good memories; except I don't remember my ranking.

Chapter 3
Dreams Came True in High School

Michael Jordan was our hero back then. We were glued to the TV whenever there was a Chicago Bulls game. The next day, we would imitate Michael Jordan's moves on the school basketball court. Because I was short, nobody wanted me to play in their games. I watched the training of the basketball team. They were tall and cool, wearing beautiful uniforms. After that, I play on the side by myself.

My father enjoyed watching the Bulls game with me as well. During weekends, we went to the basketball court together. My father used to be a basketball player. He showed and taught me how to dribble, pass and shoot. He trained me like a coach. I remember his passes were so strong. It almost knocked me off. During weekdays, I just practice dribbling and shooting by myself on the playground.

At the same time, I started to grow. Between the second and third years of junior high school, I grew fifteen cm. I grew another fifteen cm in the following year. I moved from the first row in the classroom to the last row in two years and became one of the tallest boys in the class!

One day, after class, as usual, I was practicing dribbling and shooting by myself on the side of the basketball court. I practiced with the image of Michael Jordan in my mind. Suddenly, I heard people on the basketball court shout: "You, come and play with us." I looked around but didn't see who he was talking to. "Yes, you, the tall guy. Come and play with us." One guy pointed his finger at me and shouted. "The tall guy?" I thought. Nobody had said that to me. "Come on! What are you looking at? You are dribbling well there. We are short of one person. The game is starting now!" Finally, I realised they were talking to me. For the first time in my life, I heard someone call me the tall guy and say I was dribbling well. They asked me to join their play! I was so excited and ran to join them on the court.

I had never played basketball in a team. I always played with my father one on one or by myself. I was so nervous. Once I got the ball, I looked around and I didn't know who to pass to. I had to dribble and run as fast as I could. Passed a few players and I got closer to the hoop. I did a jump shoot. The ball went in! They looked at me with the face like: "Who is this guy?" I shrugged and ran back to my position. The only thing I did that day was to dribble, run as fast as I could and shoot! I was like Forrest Gump. I never learned to play basketball in a team, but I was good at dribbling, ran fast and I could shoot. I started to play more and more with the basketball team members after school. I got along with them well. Soon, before I realised it, I joined the basketball team! I felt like my dream came true. I stood tall on the basketball court, wearing the beautiful uniform, playing with other tall guys. Girls were watching and shouting around the court. I was having the best time of my life!

I enjoyed the first two years of my senior high school. I became a star in my school. I won many awards in drawing contests.

I had a lot of influence from foreign students at the Beijing Foreign Language Institute. There were students from all around the world. My grandfather introduced me to some Russian students who studied at Beijing Foreign Language Institute near my school. I hung out with them after school. I played basketball and skateboarding with them. I was the first in school to have a skateboard when nobody knew what it was. I first saw jeans with holes in them. I dubbed audio tapes of Michael Jackson, Madonna and Prince. The Russian student gave me a Walkman. Every morning when I bicycled to school for thirty minutes, I hung it around my neck and listened to the songs of Michael Jackson.

My early venture into fashion design: Just do it!

One day, I made some holes in my jeans and wore them to school. My teacher was shocked. She stared at me and asked: "Did you fall from your bicycle on your way to school? Do you want to go to see the doctor?"

I loved Nike so much because of the cool designs and because I felt the slogan, Just Do It spoke to me. I dreamed of having Nike shoes and sportswear, but I couldn't afford them because they were expensive. I remember we watched a teacher from Japan jogging with the AirMax One and were amazed because it cost three months of our parents' salaries to buy a pair. Watching him jogging with AirMax One was like watching someone driving a Ferrari. I went to sportswear shops to observe the logo and font of Nike and embroidered them on my jersey. I also painted a big Nike logo on a white T-shirt with oil markers. My classmates were amazed. I then designed many T-shirts for The Asian Game.

At that time, we were supposed to wear the same jersey uniform to go to school. It was bulky and uncool. We hated it. I took some design clues from Japanese brands such as Asics and Mizuno and created my own design for school uniforms. Many classmates loved it, but the school didn't adopt it.

The movie Breakdance created a phenomenon among young people in China. Many kids were imitating the fashion and moves of Ozone and Turbo. I immediately picked it up by watching the VHS tapes over and over and practising on every smooth floor I could find. A few of us became very good and got to dance at our school festival.

In the early 80s in China, I could smell freedom in the air. I did exactly as my father suggested and lived a life of variety. I grew thirty centimetres in two years. As I continued to do more push-ups, I became one of the tallest and strongest in my school. My confidence grew more and more. I became the pioneer of many new things and new fashions. I felt like an ugly duckling that finally became a swan!

Chapter 4
Gave Up Dreams, Went for the Money

A dream came true?

However, the good times only lasted for two years. Soon I entered the dark ages.

In 1989, when I was in my second year of senior high school, the Tiananmen Massacre happened. Suddenly, all the freedom was taken away. My jeans and T-shirts were forbidden at school. My father took my music tapes away and burned them. I decided to shave my head to protest silently. I collected the burned tapes and carefully glued them together. I put together half of a song of Madonna, hid it secretly in my drawer and listened to it occasionally when my father was not at home. I had to face the reality.

In the following year, I entered the notorious exam preparation era. I had to stop all extra activities and focus only on cramming the exams.

I felt I was jailed for two years. The days were always dark.

I also disagreed about my future college major with my family. My father and grandfather wanted me to major in engineering. However, I wanted to pursue design, such as fashion or interior design, because I wanted to combine my passion for design with practical application to improve people's lives. I was stubborn. My family finally gave up and agreed.

I struggled with exams. I felt like it was torture. Finally, with mediocre scores, I got into a mediocre college in Beijing that pioneered a major in fashion design. However, I was happy because I got to do what I was passionate about. I smelled freedom again. I was excited about my new life during the first few weeks in college. I had long hair, wore my holed jeans again and carried a sketching board around my shoulders. I stopped from place to place in Beijing to draw people's daily lives. I dreamed of becoming a designer who could run fashion shows in Paris, Milano, New York and Tokyo.

One day, our class visited a textile factory near a suburb of Beijing. I saw lines of machine after machine weaving threads into cloth. The machines were old, heavy, covered with dust and made great noise so much so that we couldn't hear each other. All the workers were women. They all wore uniforms and white hats. After a bell rang at noon, all the women stopped working and rushed to the dining hall for lunch. I felt I saw flocks of sheep. There was only one guy who wore a pair of glasses who came and greeted us. Our teacher said: "He is your alumnus. You will be working like him in factories like this around the country." "What? I thought we were supposed to design garments?" I asked. "No. You will be designing textiles and machines that make textiles." The teacher answered. I stood there, looking at the dusty machines and white hat "sheep"; my fashion design dream bubble suddenly burst.

At that time in China, all the universities and colleges were public. The moment we entered college, we became public workers. Not only did we not have to pay tuition, but also, we received a "salary" of sixteen yuan per month. After graduation, we had no freedom to choose jobs. Our lives belonged to the country. We must go to work wherever the government sent us. That's why the "Guanxi", the connection, was especially important because, with proper connection in the government, one could go to more favourable places than others.

I was disillusioned. Didn't know what to do for a while. At that time, some of my classmates were busy doing business. There was one guy who stood out especially. He always carried a "pocket bell", a small device that receives and displays only two lines of text messages. His pocket bell rang during classes. Between classes, he usually ran out of class and made phone calls. He said on the phone, "Yes, twenty tons of steel? Two Boeing 747? OK, let me try to sort it out!" We had no idea whether he was doing some real business or showing off his special connection. Somehow, he seemed rich. He came to school sometimes by taxi and wore flashy suits.

In the early 90s, China was starting economic reform. Private companies were allowed. Under the famous slogan by Deng Xiaoping, "Be it a black cat or a white cat, it's a good cat as long as it can catch mice." "Allow some to get rich first." Capitalism was on the rise. Early adopters were trying to figure out how to make quick money. We saw some people quickly become rich, driving cars worth years of salaries for normal people.

However, most of our classmates, including myself, were poor. Our parents were all government workers. Their salaries were about three hundred yuan, or sixty dollars a month. There was a term "万元户", meaning a household earned ten thousand yuan yearly (two thousand dollars). It's the symbol of wealth. McDonald's and KFC just got into China a few years ago. People lined up to experience American fast food. A Big Mac was about twenty yuan. It was more than our monthly salary. Some of our classmates started working part-time at McDonald's and KFC. They wiped floors, washed dishes and earned six yuan per hour. Some washed cars in icy winter and earned ten yuan per hour. I felt I could do something better.

Started my first venture in Zhongguancun, the Silicon Valley of China

At that time, another magic word was the computer. Everybody was talking about computers. Some of our rich classmates even bought personal computers at home. I knew nothing about computers and went to the bookstore to find books and magazines to learn about computers. I often stood there and read for hours.

I found a part-time job in my mum's company. My mum was transferred from the Education Department to a company that imports and exports educational publications. I worked in the warehouse to package and ship books and magazines. My cousin also did a part-time job there. We were amazed by the colourful and beautiful paper of foreign magazines imported from overseas. Chinese books and magazines used paper that was not white and the texture was not smooth. They looked ugly compared to the imported magazines. We were especially interested in computer-related magazines; they were beautiful and had the latest information about hardware and software. We spent hours after school in the warehouse to work, read and discuss computers.

Our family lived in Zhongguancun, a street on the Northwest side of Beijing, stretching between Beijing University and Tsinghua University. Now it's known as the Silicon Valley of China. In the early 90s, small shops that sold computer parts started to pop up. Lianxiang, Stone, those big and famous tech companies nowadays, were just small shops on the street back then.

One day, my cousin and I came up with this brilliant idea: "Why don't we sell the beautiful, imported computer magazines with the latest information to the computer shops in Zhongguancun?" I asked the salesperson in my mum's company. He gave us the order sheets and told us to fill up the form once we got orders.

We were so excited! We quickly printed our business cards "超群电脑公司" Excellent Computer Company. Our titles were both sales managers. We decided that each of us would start knocking on doors from one end of the street of Zhongguancun. In the end, we would meet in the middle. Dressed in suits, packed three sample magazines in a briefcase and off we knocked on the doors of Zhongguancun! Initially, I was nervous and didn't know what to say. During lunch, we exchanged our sales talk and success experiences. After lunch, we started knocking on doors again. There were a couple of hundred shops on that street. It took us about a week to sweep all of them. Amazingly, we got about ten orders! The next month, we delivered the new magazines to our customers, knocked on more doors and got more orders. In order to sell the magazines, we read the content of the magazines before sales. Day in and day out, we could talk the technical language to the computer companies. Because we visited every shop on the street, we started to understand the businesses of the companies. Most of them were specialised in some parts of the computer. Some shops specialised in monitors, some in printers, some in motherboards, some in memory, some in keyboards, some in software.

One day, a customer asked us: "Do you only sell computer magazines? Do you have computer memory? We want to buy some memory." We looked at each other and said: "Yes, we do. Tell us the specs, number and price and we will find it for you." We left the shop with the specs of the memory; we started searching for the memory and compared prices in other shops. Finally, we made our first trade. Buy low, sell high; we just did it intuitively.

Soon we found out the beauty of selling magazines was its steady income. Because the magazines' subscription provided us with a steady stream of cash flow, we had free time to buy and sell computer parts in Zhongguancun. We ran around the street every day. We became savvy about the pricing of all computer parts.

I lived with my parents in a three-bedroom apartment. I stocked computer parts in my room. I pulled a phone line into my room. The phone number I put on my business card was the phone number of my home. I glued advertising flyers on utility poles all over the street. We never knew how much money we made because there was account receivable, account payable and inventory.

However, we had about four thousand yuan in our bank account. We rode taxis every day. We had pocket bells that rang all the time.

I stopped going to school. Forget about fashion design. Running a small business and making money was so much fun!

人无远虑必有近忧 If one gives no thought to a long-term plan, worries will soon appear

One day, in the middle of a business call in my room, my father came back from work and furiously broke into my room. Holding a flyer, he shouted at me, "What's going on?! You are not going to school. You put our home phone number all over the street. Strangers called and come to our home all the time!" I answered: "I am running my business. Look, I am making ten times more money than you do." "Making money? Do you know how much money you are making? You are happy with the money you are making now. How long can you do this? Do you know what you are going to do in ten years? Still like this? Running around the street, buying and selling computer parts? What if the big companies start doing what you do? What if other entrepreneurs compete with you and cut the price? You are not a businessman; you are just a small merchant. An ancient Chinese says: 'If one gives no thought to a long-term plan, worries will soon appear'. Think about your future." I stood there and started imagining. I saw myself running a small shop exactly as my father said in ten years. However, I couldn't imagine anything bigger. I realised my father was right. I felt I had the entrepreneurial drive to seize opportunities and make money quickly. However, I didn't have the vision, knowledge and business network to achieve a bigger ambition.

I went into an aguish mode for a period again.

Finally, I told my father I made the wrong decision to study fashion design. I tasted the joy of running a small business. However, I didn't want to keep selling computer parts, competing in price with other small businesses like mine. I wanted to build a big company like Legend and make an impact on people's lives. To do this, I need knowledge and experience overseas. I wanted to drop off fashion design school in China and study business overseas.

Chapter 5
Way to Japan, Survival Game

Going to Japan

Now I have a new goal, going abroad to study business.

The most popular country for Chinese students was the United States. I asked around about how to go study in the US. No one around me had that experience. The rumour about the method was to pass the TOEFL test with a high score first and write letters to US universities and have the professor invite you to attend the school. I stopped selling computer parts and started focusing on studying TOEFL and researching universities in the library. There were two thick directories of universities in the US. They were like the yellow page phone books of the universities in the US. Each page had a university with the names of professors and their addresses. I had no idea about any of the names. I decided to write to all of them one by one, starting with one letter per day. I stopped going to fashion design school. I spend all my time in the library, either studying TOEFL or writing letters to professors in the directory.

Day in and day out, half of a year passed. I had some progress in my TOEFL scores, although still far from college level; however, I got no response from any of the professors I sent letters to. I didn't know how long this would continue. Again, I felt I was living in dark days with no hope.

One day, I went to see my grandfather at his home. A

guest was talking to him. My grandfather introduced him to me, saying he was one of his students. He went to Japan and was teaching at a university in Japan. His name was Mr. Jin. Mr. Jin asked me what I was doing. I told him I had dropped off fashion design school and was working on going to study in the US. However, after six months, there was no response. I had no clue if I would get any response ever. Mr. Jin asked me, "Do you want to go to Japan?" I told him Japan was never on my radar screen. I didn't know the language; I didn't know anything about Japan. Mr. Jin told me, "Why don't you think about it? If you want to go to Japan. I can help you." That night I couldn't sleep. I started to think about everything about Japan that related to me. My father went to Japan twice on business trips. Thanks to that, all the electronics in our home were bought by him from his trips to Japan: a twenty-four-inch colour TV, a VHS video deck, a double deck cassette recorder radio and an autofocus camera. The coolest thing he bought me was a pencil case with many doors and buttons. By pushing the buttons, different doors popped open. I remember he told me about all those amazing things he saw in Japan, Disney land, telephones without dial rings, elevator doors closing fast, taxi doors opening automatically... I thought about all the cartoons I watched on TV which were from Japan, The Atom Boy, The White Lion, Ikkyu, etc. I realised that Japan already had a lot of influence on my life. I started to imagine myself studying and living in Japan. The next morning, I ran to the bookstore and picked up a Japanese language textbook (中日交流标准日本语) for the first time in my life. The characters looked Chinese. I felt an unknown confidence and hope in my heart. Yes, I can do it!

Immediately, I went to see my grandfather. I asked him to ask Mr. Jin to help me to go to Japan.

Three months later. I got good news! Mr. Jin enrolled me in a Japanese language school and got me a visa to Japan!

My family was full of joy! However, we soon realised the tuition was four hundred and fifty thousand JPY. That was about twenty-five thousand RMB. My parents were making about six hundred RMB monthly. Only the tuition was more than three years of my household income. A one-way ticket to Japan costs three thousand five hundred RMB. Not to mention there were other living expenses and future tuition.

We had a family meeting again. My grandfather and my father did the calculation. Adding all the savings between my grandfather and father, we had about seven thousand RMB. We needed to borrow twenty-two thousand RMB from others to make up for the gap. My father said he knew a friend who started doing business a few years earlier and made some money. He could borrow money from his friend. The next day, my father took me to his friend's home. I didn't remember what they were talking about. I only remember I was looking down at the floor. I couldn't look at the faces of my father and his friend. At last, my father and I bowed to his friend and thanked him, walked out of his home with an envelope, thick and heavy. There were twenty-two thousand RMB in it. My father handed it to me and said, "This is all we can do for you. Once you are in Japan, you must do it alone." It was the heaviest envelope I had ever taken in my hands. Not only was the amount of money inside beyond anything I had handled, but it also carried the hope and trust of all my family members.

We walked home in silence. I didn't know what to say. I felt guilty for putting my father in a situation where he had to borrow money from his friend for me. All the memories about my father flashed back: one push-up a day; buying me a green bicycle; practicing basketball together; encouraging me to be a happy number two; angry but yielded for me to go to fashion design school; shouting at me about my future when I sold computer parts… I realised my father's love for me. He was strict with me, like a teacher or a boss. However, he always helped me to grow. No matter what I wanted to do, he always respected my choice, even if he disagreed. He used all his resources to support me in achieving my dreams.

Finally, it's time to say goodbye to my family. We had a farewell banquet at my grandparents' place. When people were busy cooking and preparing, my grandmother pulled me into her bedroom and closed the door. She grabbed my hand and stuck three hundred dollars in it. She said to me with tears in her eyes: "I can't take care of you anymore when you are in Japan. Please take care of yourself. If, in any case, you can't live there anymore. Just use this to buy a ticket and come home. We are always here waiting for you." I cried: "Grandma… Don't worry. I will be fine. I will come back and see you soon…"

It was the first time I got on an airplane and the first time I left China for a foreign country.

On 11 May, 1993, at the age of twenty, I landed at Narita Airport in Japan with a suitcase. I didn't know what to bring. Besides clothes and textbooks, I brought a frying pan, a roll of toilet paper and a couple of instant noodles.

It was about 9pm at night. However, I was shocked that everywhere was bright when I got off the express train at Shinjuku Station. The train station was so big and full of people. I didn't know if it was day or night. I didn't know I was on the ground or underground. Mr. Jin couldn't pick me up himself. He asked a friend to pick me up and send me to a dormitory of his friend's company to stay there for a week.

The next day, I met Mr. Jin. He told me: "Japan is different from China. Everyone depends on himself. You don't have family and friends here to rely on. I can only help you to a certain degree. You must learn to survive by yourself."

I found an old apartment in Numabukuro within a week through a classmate's introduction. He was living in the building next to mine. The rent was twenty-nine thousand yen per month. The wooden two-storey apartment was built right after World War II. There were four rooms on each floor. Each of the rooms was a box with the size of six tatamis (about eleven square metres). There was a small sink and a space for one gas stove. Other than that, there was nothing in the room. There was no toilet in the rooms, only one at the end of the hallway. There was no shower room in the building. There was no bed, chair, or table, nothing but four walls, a window, a door and a tatami floor. The building was so old. Every time I climbed the stairs to get to my room on the second floor, the whole building shook and creaked. The walls were so thin I could hear the person next-door snoring at night. The first night I moved in, the room had no light bulb. In the darkness, I slept on the tatami in a sleeping bag with my suitcase beside me.

Mr. Jin's friend Mr. Fujii helped me to find a part-time job. I started washing dishes in a restaurant, Mozu, in Harajuku. Harajuku is the most popular place for young people in Tokyo. It's the centre of fashion. Mozu is an international restaurant located behind the famous toy store Kiddy Land. When I first got introduced to the manager and the chief of the Mozu, I didn't speak much Japanese. After a short conversation between them, they decided to take me on. I remember the manager was very muscular. He was tan and had long and curly hair over his shoulders. He looked scary. Later I learned he was a retired pro boxer. We all called him Chief; the chief chef was older, in his late 40s. He looked kind and was always smiling.

My personal finance: squeeze every penny

My hourly rate was eight hundred yen. I worked from 3:30pm to 11pm every day for seven and a half hours. I worked as many days in a month as possible. I could earn as much as one hundred and fifty thousand yen a month. That was seven thousand five hundred RMB! Almost "ten thousand-yuan-household" in a month! I felt rich. However, when I did the maths, I found out that I was far from making ends meet. I had to save for the four hundred and fifty-thousand-yen tuition for the next six-month term, starting in September. Having arrived in May, I only had three months to save that amount. On top of that, I needed to pay for the twenty-nine-thousand-yen monthly rent and my daily consumption, such as food and clothes. It meant my earnings from washing dishes for the next three months could only pay the tuition. I didn't have enough money to pay for anything else. It was almost impossible to save that much money. The only possibility was to work as many hours as possible to make more money and reduce spending to nearly nothing. I told Chief that I didn't need any rest. At the same time, I decided to cut down my personal consumption to as little as possible. Because the restaurant provided one meal in the evening, I just needed to eat once during the day. I found the cheapest solution: I bought one loaf of bread sliced in eight pieces and a dozen eggs, together they were about three hundred yen. They were my food for a week. My food budget was one thousand two hundred yen a month. At the beginning of the week, I boiled a dozen eggs with salt and kept them for the whole week. Every morning. I packed two eggs and one slice of bread in a bento box for school. The school was from 9am to 1pm. I ate the eggs and bread for lunch. There was a vending machine in the school. A can of juice was one hundred yen. I saw other students put in a one-hundred-yen coin and buy juices. However, one hundred yen was a third of my weekly food budget for me. It was too expensive for me. I always drank water from the hose in the washroom. The tap water in Japan was drinkable anyway.

Since the apartment had no shower room, I had to go to a public bath nearby. The public bath cost three hundred yen. It was the equivalent of my weekly food budget! I limited myself to one bath per week. For the days I didn't go to a bath, I used water and a towel to wipe my body. Once a week, I indulged in the hot bath thoroughly. It was the most luxurious moment. I spent hours in it and didn't want to leave.

Another necessity was a haircut. I found a haircut in Japan was too expensive; it usually cost three thousand to four thousand yen for a haircut. I decided not to cut my hair so that I could put together a ponytail. That'd save all haircut costs.

My part-time job, washing dishes

It was my favourite time after school, between 1pm and 3pm, to learn about Japan. I always wondered about department stores or electronic stores near Ikebukuro and Harajuku stations. BicCamera, Tobu, Seibu, Kiddy Land and Tokyu Hands were like Disney lands for me. There were so many gadgets I had never seen before. The best part was that I could play with them freely. At 3:30pm, I arrived at the restaurant, changed into a white uniform and started preparing materials for dinner opening at 5pm.

Since I wasn't good at Japanese, the cooks would show me what they wanted me to do and let me do it. I washed vegetables, cut vegetables, boiled spaghetti and broke and scrambled eggs.

After the restaurant opened at 5pm, some customers started to enter the shop. All the cooks started getting busy cooking. I started washing dishes. Waiters brought orders in on paper slips. They stuck the slips under a rubber band at the counter of the kitchen. The main part of the kitchen was open to the hall. There was a big hot steel plate where chefs cooked Teppanyaki in front of the customers. There was a big counter behind the hot steel plate. Behind the counter were many gas stoves where most of the food was cooked. There were two to three chefs there cooking.

At the other end of the kitchen, there was a small room. It was the area for washing, cutting and storage. A couple of chefs were there cutting and preparing for the food to be cooked.

I was the only person who washed the dishes. There was a counter where the waiters carried and piled the dishes. Behind the counter, there were two big sinks made of stainless steel. One sink was full of warm water with detergent. The other sink was full of clean water. Next to the sinks, there was a dishwashing machine. My job was first to wash the dishes in the sink with detergent. Then rinse them in the sink with clean water. Then I put the dishes in the washing machine and let it run for ten minutes. The washing machine used very hot water to clean the dishes and dry them thoroughly. Finally, I picked the hot plates from the washing machine and supplied them to the main kitchen or placed them in storage.

We got really busy the first Friday when I started working at the restaurant. One side of the counter was full of paper-slip orders. Dishes were piling up in front of me as well. Waiters came many times to ask if the dishes were ready. Chefs were running around in the kitchen to catch up with the orders. I kept washing and washing. The dishes just kept piling up.

Suddenly, one of the chefs cooking in the main kitchen shouted at me. It was my first week in Japan. I didn't understand what he was saying. It seemed he wanted me to get him some material or ingredients from the storage area. I stood there and had no clue what he was saying.

After repeating it a couple of times, he gave up, rushed to the storage area and grabbed some vegetables himself. He shook his head while passing by me. I felt I was useless. I decided to learn about all the names of vegetables and ingredients in the kitchen. I spend the whole day in a supermarket near my apartment at the weekend. I wrote down all the names of vegetables on a notepad in Japanese and Chinese. The second day, when I was writing down the names of the ingredients in the same supermarket, the store manager came to me and asked me what I was doing. I showed him my notepad. He smiled and left.

The following week, I got in the kitchen and could say all the names of the vegetable in Japanese.

I love my job at the restaurant because they provide a meal. Before opening at around 5pm, chefs cooked a special meal for the chefs and waiters. It was the only full meal I had in a day. I ate as much as I could. However, I was twenty years old. After washing dishes for hours, later in the night, I got hungry. I found some food left by the customers on the plates piled on the counter. Waiters threw the food away into the garbage bin under the counter. I told them: "You don't need to do it. Just leave the plates on the counter. I will do it." They thanked me and left. I picked up some leftover food and ate when nobody was watching. One day, a big piece of meat was left on the plate. The waiter was talking to a chef around me. I was so hungry looking at the meat. I was swallowing my saliva. However, with people around, I had to dump it in the garbage bin. After they left, I quickly picked the meat up from the garbage bin and put it in my mouth.

Cutting, cutting and cutting

One afternoon, I got the job of cutting onions. I never saw so many onions in my life. They were piling up on the kitchen counter like a small mountain. The chef showed me how to peel the onion skin and cut it into small pieces using a knife. As I kept cutting, tears started coming out of my eyes. There were too many onions. Tears blurred my eyesight. I couldn't wipe tears with my hands either. I had to look up or let the tears run down my face. It was even hard to breathe. However, facing the mountain of onions, I couldn't stop cutting.

Suddenly, I felt a shocking pain from the pointing finger of my left hand. It was beyond any pain I had ever experienced. I felt I was electrified. The sharp pain ran from my finger through my left arm. My whole body was trembling. I immediately unconsciously grabbed my finger using my right hand. Blood was running through the fingers of my right hand. I realised I had cut my finger and it was very bad. I held my finger tightly to stop bleeding. I looked down at the cutting board and through my blurred sight, I saw a piece of meat with fingernails lying on it among the chopped onions.

My mother's face bubbled up in front of me at that moment. She was silently smiling at me with kindness. I felt a different kind of tear rushing out of my eyes. It was hot and salty. I felt like I was zoomed out as if someone was looking at me from a thousand metres from the sky. I felt I was so small. Stuck in a kitchen filled with onions among millions of buildings in Tokyo, thousands of miles from my home, Beijing, I was helpless and powerless.

What am I doing here? Why?

I felt my mother must be thinking about me at that moment. She didn't know what was happening to me. Even she knew she couldn't help me. She could only look at me and smile. Her smile was so gentle, but it gave me strength. I remembered how hard I tried to come to Japan. Scenes of my father borrowing money, my grandfather encouraging me to attend college in Japan and my grandmother handing me the dollars quickly flashed in front of me. I swallowed tears and calmed down. I knew it was me who decided to come to Japan. It was I who decided to survive by myself. It's only my second week in Japan. I still have a long way to go.

Quickly I looked around. The chefs were busy working in the main kitchen. Nobody noticed me. I immediately realised I shouldn't tell them about my accident. Otherwise, they would make me stop working for days or even fire me. Then I will lose my only source of income.

Holding my finger, I managed to get the first-aid box from the shelf and took some plasters out. I decided to wrap it up myself without telling anyone. I knew the blood would gush out if I let my hand go, but I had no choice. I quickly released my right hand and reached out to the plasters. As expected, the cut was big and blood was gushing out of the wound. I quickly put one, two, three, or four plasters around my finger and held it until the bleeding stopped. Gritting my teeth, enduring the pain, I went back to cutting onions. I could finish all the preparation work thanks to nobody paying attention to me.

At around 6pm, customers started to come. I transitioned into the dishwashing job. The dishes started to pile up. How can I put my wounded hand into the water? I found a small plastic bag, wrapped it around my finger and dipped my hands into the water. It was fine initially; however, as time passed, the detergent started to penetrate the plastic bag. I started to feel the pain in my finger, like mice chewing on it. I kept gritting my teeth. Sweat and tears mixed in my eyes and dropped from my face. After a while, I became numb to the pain. I felt I was like a robot, repeating the same movement over and over. "Are you OK?" Chief stood next to me. He saw my finger wrapped in a plastic bag. Obviously, he realised something was not right. "It's a small cut. No big deal at all." I squeezed a smile and tried to cover my finger. "Are you sure? Do you want to rest for a couple of days?" "No, no need at all. I am fine." "OK then." Chief returned to the main kitchen. I breathed hard by myself, thinking I had to do this for the rest of the night and many more days.

I didn't know how many dishes I washed that night. I kept telling myself, one dish at a time. I remembered the push-ups I was doing with my father. One push-up a day. Yes, it was painful, but I will never let my family be disappointed. I will do it. I can do it!

Finally, it was over. I got home. Looking at my finger, I saw the plasters were soaked with detergent and were dirty. I had to take them off, sanitise the wound and wrap my finger up with clean plasters. I knew it was going to be painful. I happened to have a small bottle of hard liquor from China, Erguotou, with fifty-four degrees of alcohol. I poured it into a glass. I took a deep breath, gulped half the liquor and quickly tore the plaster off my finger. Ahh! I shouted. Ouch! With acute pain, blood gushed out again. I quickly dip my finger into the glass. Ahhhh! I shouted again. It was even more painful! The glass quickly became red. I pulled my finger out and quickly wrapped it with some clean plasters. It was so painful that I drank the whole glass of liquor with blood at once. I was breathing hard. My eyes were full of sweat and tears again.

Loneliness is more painful

I quickly found out I was a rare type at the language school. I was among the 90 per cent of the students who came from mainland China. We all had to do part-time jobs. Some even did two or three part-time jobs. There were few students from Taiwan and Korea. They were rich and didn't have to do part-time jobs.

Most Chinese students were only in the language school to extend their visas. We held a "pre-college" visa. I needed to renew my visa every six months at the immigration office. Pre-college visa could only be extended for a maximum of two years. The immigration office could only extend the visa if the school confirmed more than ninety per cent attendance.

Most of the Chinese students in my school were from rural areas of China. Their motivation was to stay in Japan as long as possible to make money by doing part-time jobs. One of my classmates told me he worked two part-time jobs washing dishes and cleaning buildings at night. He almost had no time to sleep at night. He always slept in the classes. He told me that if he worked for two years like that, he could build a small house back in his hometown and get married. Nobody was interested in getting into college and working in Japan for the long term.

I had no friends at school. I had no friends at work.

Two months passed after I arrived in Japan and the school summer break started in July. For one month, we had no school. In the morning, I studied by myself at home. At 3:30pm, I started working at the restaurant. At 11:30pm, I took the last train home.

As time went by, I realised I had had no conversation with anyone for a month. At the restaurant, I was silently washing the dishes. People knew I couldn't speak Japanese. No one talked to me. There was a small window at the back of the kitchen. I looked out and saw some young Japanese my age driving a red convertible sports car, playing music loudly. I envied them so much. I couldn't imagine how they could have the money and time to do that. They looked shining, stylish and smiling with sunglasses. I looked at myself and I was cutting vegetables and washing dishes in a dark and cold kitchen. One day, I thought, I wanted to be like them, driving a convertible car in the sunshine.

After a couple of weeks of not speaking a word to anyone, I started to doubt my existence. Am I still alive? I touched my face, looked into the mirror and spoke to myself. I thought if I died, nobody would realise until the landlord opened the door one month later when he found out I didn't pay the rent.

I had an illusion that I was an invisible man. Japanese people had no eye contact with me, even on the crowded train. I intentionally bumped into people on the street or on the train. When they looked at me, I realised I existed.

My only hope was the letters from my family and friends in China. Every day, I checked the mailbox many times to see if there were any letters. I got a couple of letters from my grandfather and friends. My friends even mailed me tapes of my favourite music. I put the tape in the recorder, which I picked from the garbage. Listening to the old songs, I cried loudly. My tears smeared the words on the letters. I realised that the loneliness was more painful than the physical pain of cutting my finger.

Study, study, study

I put all my energy into the study. My goal was to enter college by next April, when the new school year starts. To do that, I needed to pass the Japanese language level N1 test and the Central Exam, which included five subjects, all in Japanese, by December. I only had five months.

It required two thousand words to pass the N1 test. I learned about one thousand. There were one thousand more to go. I calculated that I needed to remember seven words per day to hit two thousand words by December. I put paper around my apartment and wrote seven words on the wall and on my notepad daily. On the train, I kept repeating the words. Words quickly filled up my walls.

At the restaurant, there were times with no customers for a while and no dish to wash. I took a textbook to the kitchen. When there were no customers, I squatted so nobody could see me, then I started reading. I used a pencil to write in the white spaces between the lines. When customers came, the waiters shouted, "Irasshyaimase!" (meaning welcome in Japanese). I stood up and shouted the same. When customers left, the waiters and chefs shouted, "Doumo arigatou gozaimashita!" (meaning thank you in Japanese). I quickly stood up and shouted the same. I put the textbook away and washed the dishes when the dishes came. After washing, I wiped my hands and picked up my textbook to practice again.

Day in and day out, the textbook was full of stains of oil, water and detergent. My writing was full between the lines. One day, Chief flipped through the textbook and asked me. "What are you doing?" I told him I aimed to pass the exam by the end of the year. He showed everybody in the restaurant my textbook and said, "Let's all help him practice Japanese and pass the exam!"

When there were no customers, some part-time job waiters who were college students came to my counter and taught me Japanese.

One day, they asked me where I came from. I told them about my family in Beijing. When I told them that my grandfather was a professor at a university, they all came to see me. They surrounded me and said, "We had never met a grandson of a professor in our lives!" I realised I had never met people who worked in restaurants when I was in Beijing, either. They were warm and kind to me. I started getting along well with the people in the restaurant. However, I knew I wasn't one of them.

With many hours poured into work and stoic saving, miraculously, I saved four hundred and fifty thousand yen and paid my tuition for the next term.

One day in October, I got to know that Waseda University, a top-tier university in Japan, had an early admission programme. I wanted to give it a try. However, the tuition was about one million three hundred thousand yen, beyond my capability. I called Mr. Jin and told him about the programme. "How are you going to pay the tuition, even if you got in?" he asked calmly. I got stuck. I couldn't ask him to lend me the money. "You are right... I should forget about it." I hung up the phone. I realised that back in China, I never thought about tuition. All colleges were public. My parents paid other fees. Now I had to depend on myself completely. I felt sad that I didn't even have a chance to try. Why is the world unfair? Why are some people are rich and some poor? I asked myself.

However, I quickly faced the reality. Instead of complaining, I just needed to survive.

After some research, I found out that all private universities were out of my capability. I didn't have money to pay for any of them. My only chance was to get into public universities and get an exemption for tuition.

I studied even harder. Not only did I have to study Japanese, but I also had to study maths, history, chemistry, physics and English to pass the Central Exam to get into public universities. I woke up early in the morning. I studied after coming home from eight hours of washing dishes at night. I continued studying on the train and under the counter in the kitchen.

Finally, I passed N4, N3 and N2 Japanese language tests. The school upgraded me to higher-level classes twice. When I left my class, the teacher said: "I am going to miss you because you are the only student who asks me questions."

I passed the N1 in December! Now I was qualified to go to university in Japan!

I picked up a small TV from the garbage. I always kept it turned on in the background to let Japanese fill my ears. One day, I was cleaning my apartment while leaving the TV on as usual. Suddenly, I realised I could understand the meaning. I quickly turned around and tried to listen to the TV carefully. Then I could hardly understand it. I tried to relax and not watch it. Then I could understand it again! Wow! I could understand Japanese on TV! I was so happy. Magically, I could understand almost everything in Japanese on TV! I realised I was translating Japanese into Chinese and trying to understand the meaning. However, at that moment, I didn't need to translate. I could understand Japanese as it was! I realised that learning Japanese was just like riding a bicycle or playing basketball. Once my brain and body learned how to do it, it became automatic. I didn't need to think about it.

Finally, it's time for the Central Exam. The place for Central Exam was at Waseda. I walked on the campus with difficult feelings. I knew I had no chance of getting in Waseda. However, I would do my best so that I could get into a public university and get an exemption to tuition based on my scores.

Harvest of hardwork

I was called to the headquarters office at the language school. The principal told me: "Do you know how many people were there taking the Central Exam? There were four hundred and eighty thousand people. Do you know your ranking among them?" "No," I replied. "Number fourteen!" He raised his voice and looked at me excitedly. "In the past twenty years of our history, we never had a student with this kind of ranking! Not even close!" "You made us proud!". I couldn't believe it myself. "We have decided to give you a scholarship, fifty thousand yen per month for one year for your university." It's the first time the language school had given a scholarship to a student who was graduating. Later I learned that I was one of the two students who got into college among one hundred students who graduated that year.

Mr. Jin's friend, my guarantor, Mr. Fujii, was the CEO of Ark Information Systems. He convinced his company to give me a scholarship as well for fifty thousand yen per month.

The good news continues. I got into Saitama University and got the tuition exemption! It's the public university of Saitama Prefecture. The major I applied for was Business Management in Economics Department.

With a one-hundred-thousand-yen scholarship per month and tuition exemption, I no longer needed to wash dishes.

I thought about my father's conversation with me about my small computer parts business. I finally had a chance to learn about business. My dream was coming true!

It was time to say goodbye to the people in the restaurant. I worked there for almost a year. Chief bought me a diver's watch as a gift. The waiters bought me a microwave oven. They said that since I couldn't eat at the restaurant, I could use the microwave oven to heat food myself. We hugged and wept.

UNDERSTANDING THE WAY

LU DONG

Chapter 6
Blossom in Saitama University

My new life back on campus

April 1994, eleven months after I landed in Japan. I started a new chapter in my life.

On the first day at Saitama University, I was so excited. The campus was big with much greenery. I felt familiar. It was like the campus I grew up in Beijing.

I sat in the classroom. It was bright, big and quiet, unlike the dark and cold kitchen where I spent most of my time last year. I no longer needed to squat under the counter. I could sit in the chair with my back straight. I no longer needed to read while listening to "Irasshyaimase" and stand up to go back to work. I could focus on study only. I listened to the sound of the chalk writing on the blackboard. It was musical. It was a life I dreamed about. I felt the warmth of the sun's rays on my skin. I could smell the greenery through the window. My whole body enjoyed the freedom. Never in my life had I felt studying was such a luxury thing.

I lived in a regular student dorm with Japanese students. In one room, there were four bunker beds. I was in the lower bed. There were two other Japanese students. One top bed was empty for storage.

I thought I already understood Japanese from TV. However, when I started talking to Japanese students, I ultimately couldn't understand what they were talking about. Their language was completely different from the TV or the Japanese teachers in school. I had to learn the Japanese language spoken by young people. Living with them in the same room, blending in didn't take me long.

There were about two hundred students living in the dorm. There were two buildings for males and one building for females. There was a big dining hall between the male and the female buildings. The food was cheap. It only cost one hundred and fifty yen per meal. On each floor, there was a kitchen for all students to use. I often cooked Chinese food for my dorm mates. They loved the stir-fried tomato and eggs.

There was a vast public bathroom on the first floor. I could take a hot bath every day. Another dream came true! Never in my life did I take a hot bath every day. I met another Chinese student in the dorm. He was from Nanjing. One day he earnestly told me: "I found a secret of Japanese. Unlike the Chinese, their bodies must give off something dirty that they must wash every day. Us Chinese don't need to wash every day. We only need to wash once a week." I thought he was joking, but he was serious. I realised that back in China, we were told that taking a bath once a week was the right thing.

My first dorm mates were noisy. The students never studied. They played computer games every day until late at night. I changed to another room with students who loved quiet lives. One of them was Fumihiko Yokota, who later became one of my best friends in my life.

I spent more time studying because studying was such an enjoyable experience. Also, I carried many expectations from my family. My father borrowed money to send me to

Japan. My grandfather always encouraged me to pursue a higher degree.

At school, I discovered more scholarships to apply for. After the first term, I got all A's in my grades. I won two more scholarships. Now I had two hundred thousand yen of scholarship per month. It was more than I earned when I washed dishes for eight hours daily. It was more than most Chinese make per year! I tasted the joy of studying. It was way better to make money by studying than labouring.

I returned to China to see my family during the first summer holiday.

I was so excited to tell them everything I experienced in Japan. I cooked all kinds of Japanese food I learned at the restaurant. Most importantly, I returned all the money my father borrowed from his friend. Also, I returned all the money I borrowed from all my family members. I never thought I could return the money so quickly.

Encounter the internet

After the first year, I got all A's in my classes. I was not only the top student in the Economy Department but also the top student across the university. In the second year, I entered Marketing Seminar taught by Professor Usui. Professor Usui took us to the computer lab and showed us his home page on Infomosaic, an internet browser. He also showed us that he could email students in England in real time. I was amazed by the Internet immediately. When I was selling computer parts in China, all the personal computers were not connected. With the internet, all computers could be connected. The world became borderless.

I started to take classes in the Computer Science Department. After school, I indulged in the computer lab to build websites and LAN to connect servers and clients. I learned how to connect different types of computers, such as Macintosh, SUN workstations and Windows-based PCs. I soon became a teaching assistant at the computer lab.

Founding Try Me

I also started to explore extra curriculum activities. Although there were many student clubs, I founded none of them fitted my interests. There were no clubs for international students, even though there were more than one hundred and forty international students. They were also diversified: Cambodia, Mauritania, Indonesia, Australia and many from China.

I talked with Fumi about my thought on creating a new club for international students to learn from each other. He immediately became interested in it. Fumi's uncle ran across the American continent. He always kept a picture of his uncle running. Fumi's dream was to study abroad. After talking with a few other international students, we gathered enough people and ideas to formally apply to the university to form a new student club. We named it Try Me. We felt we were ready to challenge ourselves. At the same time, we wanted more international and Japanese students to join us to explore different cultures.

The university approved the student club and we even got some funding. We got about fifty students to join us. We set the official languages used in the club to be Japanese, Chinese and English.

Becoming a society person through the NHK part-time job

Although I didn't need to do part-time jobs to earn money, I wanted to find a part-time job to learn more about Japan's society. I learned there was a word 社会人 "society persons" which means salaryman. I wondered why students were not part of society. Literally, Japanese students' lifestyle was not part of society. They studied hard in high school to get into college. After college, they would work for companies until they retired. It was almost as if the four years in college were the only long vacation they could have in their lives. That was why most students cared less about their studies. They would be re-educated by the companies after graduation anyway. They played all the time. During classes, nobody asked any questions. I always sat in the front row and asked questions.

I didn't want to be excluded from society; I wanted to be part of society.

I found a perfect job to learn deeply about Japan's society. I got a part-time job at NHK Urawa station. NHK was the national TV station, like the BBC in the UK or CCTV in China. My role was cameraman assistant in the news crew. During working hours, we sat in the office watching the news coming in and waiting for the opportunity to report. Then I learned that the news we saw on TV was only a fraction of what was happening in the real world. There were two fax machines in the news station. One was connected to the fire station. The other was connected to the police. Almost every hour, the fax machine was printing some accidents, such as a fire burning two houses or a person getting stabbed by a knife in a garage. The director of the news station checked them and picked ones for us to go reporting.

The reporting was exciting and nerve-racking. Usually, a reporter, a cameraman and a cameraman's assistant would go together as a small team. There were two cameramen at the news station. They were in their fifties. One of them had a ponytail and drove a Harley Davison to work. They had worked there for a long time. The reporters were young. They moved from station to station. The two cameramen were like the second level boss in the news station. They had unique and hard-to-please personalities. They smoked in the office with their feet on the table. When it was time for outgoing reporting, the reporters came to their desks and bent over to ask them to go. However, it was the cameraman's assistant who got scolded the most. We carried a big video camera that weighed ten kg, a tripod that weighed five kg, a backpack stuffed with batteries for the camera and many videotapes and a backpack stuffed with lights, filters, a microphone and cables. Altogether, it was about twenty kgs of gear we had to carry.

Most of the time, I had to fight for the best spot among other TV stations' crews for video shooting. In some famous incidents, I could often see myself in other TV stations' news. Despite the heavy labour, cameramen often got angry with us assistants. "Too slow!", "Wrong colour!", "No battery!", "Get out of my way!" They were rarely happy.

NHK gave us a pocket bell for urgent news reporting purposes. Sometimes I got calls at night and had to rush to the news station.

In two years, I witnessed the arresting of politicians and Yakuzas (gangsters), fires, murders and interviewed the Prime Minister. It was thrilling and fun.

Survive and success in the recruiting game

In the third year, I found a fun internship at the IT department of Barings Bank to build computer networks. For the first time, I used my computer and English skills in an international company.

The recruiting season started. All the third-year students in the dorm got a thick deck of booklets in their mailboxes. The books were company information sent by Recruit, which dominated the student recruiting market. Like most Japanese students did, I started sending postcards to apply for recruiting seminars to Japanese companies. Then I got into dark suits and started going to recruiting seminars and interviews. My dream was to do marketing. I applied to advertising companies and Japanese trading companies. After passing the written test, I got invitations to interviews. The interviews went well. I proceeded to the second and third rounds of interviews.

One day, I got a final interview with a Japanese company. A director-level person interviewed me. He looked about fifty years old. He said: "Congratulations on getting into the final interview. I heard good feedback about you. So, where are you from?" "Chugoku," I replied and felt good about his initial comment. "Oh, which part of Chugoku?" he asked. "Beijing." I replied. "You mean you are from China?" His face changed. "Yes, I am from Beijing, China." "You are Chinese?" He put on his glasses and looked at my resume. "Yes, I am," I replied. "Well, I thought you were from the Chugoku area of Japan. Why didn't you tell us earlier that you are Chinese? You know, unfortunately, we don't hire Chinese. I am sorry; what a pity. You are a perfect candidate." I realised there was a region in Japan called Chugoku. It has the same character and pronunciation as the word China. All the interviewers didn't know I was Chinese. Having lived with Japanese students in the dorm for three years, my Japanese became very good. Looking no different from Japanese, nobody could tell I was not Japanese. "Oh, OK," I replied with great disappointment. I left the company and felt powerless. They couldn't even tell I was Chinese; why didn't they give me an equal opportunity as Japanese?

Never give up! I continued interviews with other Japanese companies. The same situation repeated a couple of times. After some interviews, they found out I was Chinese, then they all said the same. "Sorry, we don't hire Chinese." Even the advertising company I dreamed about rejected me. As I continued to apply to Japanese companies and proceeded with interviews, I formed a new strategy. In the first interview, I started self-introduction by saying "I am Chinese. I am from Beijing, China." After that, I stopped and waited for their response. When the interviewer said: "su..." in Japanese means no without saying no. Then I just stood up and left. After repeating this about ten times, I realised that finding a job at a Japanese company was impossible because they didn't hire Chinese. I remembered my experience at Barings Bank. There were many foreigners. They may hire Chinese. Then I started to look for jobs in foreign companies in Japan. Many foreign companies in the finance industry had job postings from IT departments. I thought it would be an excellent opportunity to work in the IT department to learn both IT and business.

One day, I called to apply to a recruiting seminar at the Goldman Sachs Tokyo office. The HR lady on the phone asked for my name, school and major. I told her my major was economics. "Sorry," she said, "We only accept students from computer science major for the IT department." "But I studied computer science as well." "Sorry, we only accept computer science major for the IT department," she repeated. "You can apply for trading or investment banking if you are economics majored." Hung up the phone, I was disappointed. I felt rejected again, not because of what I could do but because of some labels. However, I decided to give it another try. I just wanted to prove I was equally as good as students who majored in computer science. I called them again. This time, it was a different person on the phone. "Your name, school and major, please?" "Lu Dong, Saitama University, Computer Science." I replied. "OK, you are registered for the written exam." Yes! Finally, I got a chance to prove myself.

The exam went well. I got invitations to go to interviews. One after another, I had got more than twenty interviews already. I knew it was a good sign. Finally, I got an interview with the head of the IT department.

I walked into the room. A foreign-looking man with a thick beard suggested I sit down. "Can you please introduce yourself?" He asked. "Sure. My name is Lu Dong. I am a Chinese." As usual, I stopped, looked at him and waited for his reaction. He was looking at my resume. After the silence continued for ten seconds, he looked at me and said, "So what? I am from Turkey. Continue." "Really?" I said to myself in my heart. It's cool! He didn't care that I was Chinese! I became excited. I started to tell him about my experience of coming to Japan, studying Japanese, washing dishes at a restaurant, getting scholarships at Saitama University and studying economics and computer science simultaneously. After patiently listening to me talk about my life, he finally asked, "Wow, you did a lot! So basically, you can do anything you want?" "Yes!" I eagerly replied. "As long you give me a chance," I added, "You don't have to pay me. Just let me work for one month for you. If you don't like what I do, you can fire me then." He smiled at me. "OK. You are in." Wow! That was the happiest moment of my life! I got my first job! It was at Goldman Sachs in Japan!

Numan, the Turkish guy, became my boss. He later told me I was the only one hired to his team that year among four hundred candidates who all majored in computer science. I had twenty-five interviews. Every interviewer needed to rate the candidate from one to three. One meant not good. Two meant mediocre and three meant good. To be hired, the candidate must receive three from all twenty-five interviewers. I felt I was so lucky.

My dream of working in Japan finally came true! And it was one of the best companies in the world! My starting salary was about double that of my peers who worked in Japanese companies. I made copies of my offer letter and sent them to my father and grandfather.

LU DONG

Chapter 7
Learnings and Struggles at Goldman Sachs

Question: what value does GS create?

On the first day working in the Goldman Sachs Japan office, about 30 new associates gathered in a big meeting room of one of the most prestigious office buildings in Tokyo. We began the two-week orientation with an opening speech by the CEO of Goldman Sachs Japan, the head of investment banking.

After he gave us a thirty-minute speech, all the new associates were silent, just as the students were silent in classes at my university. "I have a question." I raised my hand with a Nikkei newspaper in the other hand. "Today's Nikkei article says Goldman Sachs Japan just got fined by the government. Can you please tell us what value Goldman Sachs creates for society?" Everybody stared at me with strange looks. "What's wrong with this guy?"

I didn't think there was anything wrong. From when I was a child, I remember my grandfather always telling me to ask him tough questions. "There are no stupid questions, only stupid answers." I always had questions about the meaning and purpose of the banking industry. It just happened that there was news about Goldman Sachs being fined by Japan's government on the same day as the first day of my work at Goldman Sachs.

"Well, good question." The CEO paused for a few seconds and answered. "Our society is like a human body. Different industries are like different organs: the steel industry is like bones; the automobile industry is like legs and the agriculture industry is like a stomach. Investment banking is like the blood. We provide liquidity to all the industries so that they can function better." It was a good answer. I sat down but was still not entirely convinced.

During the break, a well-built new associate guy whispered to me. "You were saucy." "Really? I was just curious," I said. Then we started chatting. His name was Akira Saito. Later, he became one of my best friends for over twenty years.

Goldman Sachs had fourteen principles when I joined in 1998. (*See attachment. https://www.goldmansachs.com/our-firm/history/moments/1979-business-principles.html*) I resonate with a lot of them. The ones I liked the most were Number three, number five and number ten. During the orientation training, the HR person kept telling us, we are the best; we selected you because you are the best. We are going to train you to be the best. You need to work hard to ensure you are the best, meaning your work has to be better than your peer at Morgan Staley, Merrill Lynch, Deutsche Bank and all other banks.

"If it comes to a choice, rather be best than biggest." I held great pride in that phrase because I knew Goldman Sachs was the smallest among the Big Three Wall Street firms. I was proud of being the best rather than the biggest.

I always have a habit of questioning the meaning of what I do. "Why…" I always thought.

There was nothing about conservativeness in the fourteen principles. However, one of the HR people told us during the orientation training. "If you don't know what to do. Don't do it." I didn't understand why. One of the slogans that always motivated me was, "Just do it!" Unless you do it, you never know whether it's right or wrong, I thought.

In most cases, I felt Goldman Sachs did precisely what the fourteen principles said. For example, Goldman Sachs defined people as one of the most essential assets in principle number two. In principle number five, it said, "without the best people, we cannot be the best firm". Goldman Sachs put a lot of effort and cost into recruiting and training. During the orientation, an HR person showed us the Equity trading floor. There were many open seats. Each seat was set up with a phone, a computer and a Herman Miller Aeron chair. "Do you know how much this chair cost?" The HR person asked. "Three thousand dollars." Wow! We were all shocked. "Do you know how much money we spend to recruit and train a person to sit on this chair?" The HR person continued. "Three hundred thousand dollars." The number was just too shocking. My starting salary was fifty thousand dollars. It's six years my salary! How can the firm make profits? A few months later, during my training in New York, I understood how they spent three hundred thousand to train one new associate.

The other thing I was shocked to learn was right after the two-week-long new orientation, we were told to start helping to recruit. I thought recruiting was HR's job or jobs for someone senior in the company instead of new associates. We barely knew how everything worked at

Goldman Sachs. We were sent to mingle with the students in a recruiting seminar. "It's easy, just pick the ones you would like to work with. Remember their names and let us know." The HR person told us. I followed the instruction. To my surprise, those who we agreed that we liked got hired the following year.

The most exciting part of the training was joining the new associate training programme in New York! It started in July and lasted for six months. For the first time, I got on a plane in business class. They put me in an apartment in Battery Park City. I couldn't believe my eyes when I walked into the apartment. It was a two-bedroomed, one hundred and twenty-square-metre apartment with a vast living room. I could see the twin towers of the World Trade Center from the window of the living room and the Statue of Liberty from my bedroom. I had only a forty-square-metre studio back in Tokyo.

There were about three hundred new associates from our global offices for the training. They put us on the top floors of the World Trade Center, Windows on the World. They were on the 106th and 107th floors of the North Tower of WTC. For two weeks, we had training courses with speakers from different departments of Goldman Sachs. Every day, three meals were served on round tables with full courses. We could see planes flying below the level of our floor from the windows.

I remember one training course was about dress manners. The trainer told us what kind of suits, shirts, ties and shoes we should wear. We were told never to roll up our sleeves or wear short-sleeved shirts. Always shine our shoes. We should never put a pen under fifty dollars in the shirt's pocket.

Every night, parties were held in the most incredible places in New York City. I remember one was on a cruiser on the Hudson River; one was at the most famous club, The Web. One was at the Lincoln Center.

Everyone was amazed. We were in our early twenties. We never saw anything like that. It was like in the movies. We felt we were on top of the world. We thought we were the best.

All new associates were given a canvas bag with Goldman's logo on it. We were so proud of putting that bag on our shoulders when we walked around the city. It was the season of training newcomers on Wall Street. We saw young people wearing suits and holding similar canvas bags with different logos: Morgan Stanley, JP Morgan and Merrill Lynch. I felt I was the best because my bag said Goldman Sachs. Whenever I met some girls in bars and showed them my business card, I always got the look in their shining eyes: "Wow! Goldman Sachs!" That made me feel special and I enjoyed that feeling.

Work hard, play hard!

Work hard, play hard was our slogan. We were trained in computers and IT systems during the day. I studied at night to pass Series Seven, worked out in the gym and partied until the morning often. I enjoyed rollerblading in Central Park, sunbathing on the Long Island beach and BBQ on Bear Mountain during weekends. Six months went by quickly. My memories of the six months of training in New York were like the DiCaprio movie, The Wolf of Wall Street.

Back in Tokyo, I continued to work hard and play hard. I loved the culture of Goldman Sachs. Everybody was kind and generous to teach and help me. As a new associate, I had a lot of questions. There were just too many things I didn't know or understand. Whenever I had a question, anyone I asked would always stop their work and start to explain or teach me, I was touched and thought I would do the same for others. We got along so well as a family. After work, we always went drinking together in Roppongi near our office.

Community Teamwork

Goldman Sachs' training programme was like an MBA programme. We could get training in the office even during office hours, if we got the approval from our managers. I applied and got training in various areas, such as presentation skills, negotiation skills and active listening. Even as a new associate, I got into a training course on leadership skills. My boss always encouraged me to go to the training courses. I learned so much.

Besides work, I especially enjoyed the training and Community Teamwork at the Goldman Sachs' Tokyo office. Community Teamwork was a volunteer system. There was a calendar with different volunteer programmes on the intranet to which everyone in the company could apply. Some were on the weekends and some were on weekdays. Again, the rules were that one could apply to as many as possible as long as the manager approved. I was a single guy with a lot of energy. I applied to many programmes, such as teaching basketball to special Olympic children, taking old people in the facility to the zoo and cleaning Komazawa park in Tokyo. After one day of volunteer work, I got a colourful flag with the Community Teamwork logo on it. The flags were on a stand to be put on the desks. After one year, I had the greatest number of flags on my desk in the IT department. Community Teamwork also gave me opportunities to interact with people from different departments such as Equity, Fixed Income, Investment Banking and back offices. I made many friends and learned a lot about their businesses.

One day in the second year after I joined Goldman Sachs, one event of Community Teamwork gave me a great shock that changed my attitude.

I took a day off to take the old people from the facility to a safari park near Tokyo. We used a small bus to carry them during the day. One of the old ladies was in a wheelchair. Whenever she had to get on the bus, I held her from the wheelchair and put her in a seat on the bus, carried the wheelchair on the bus and folded the wheelchair. Whenever she needed to get off the bus, I carried the wheelchair off the bus, unfolded it, got on the bus, carried the old lady in my arms, got off the bus and put her in the wheelchair. During the trip, I did this many times. I treated her as my grandmother. She was frail. She couldn't walk or speak. Finally, the trip ended at the end of the day. We drove them back to the facility. I put her in the wheelchair and said goodbye. Suddenly, she grabbed my hand, put a key ring in my hand and held my hands tightly. Although she couldn't speak, she looked at me, tears running out of her eyes.

I looked at the keyring. It was an elephant made of cloth. I didn't understand what she meant. One of the caretakers in the facility explained that the old lady made the keyring by herself. Suddenly, I was touched and tears also came out of my eyes. I saw my grandmother in the old lady. She couldn't say anything, but she gave me this keyring she used all her strength to make. It was a symbol of her love. She gave it to me because I gave her love. I recalled when my grandmother grabbed my hands and put all her savings in my hands before I left China.

I felt like I was falling from the cloud to the ground and humbled back to a boy who grew up in a poor family in Beijing.

After my flashy experience in New York, branded with Goldman Sachs, the most prestigious Wall Street firm, working among the youngest, brightest and wealthiest people in Tokyo, I was proud of myself. Although I was volunteering for old people, I wasn't doing it for the people. I was doing it for myself. I was doing it for the ego that I not only was the top achiever at work but also was a top performer in volunteer work. However, the old lady didn't know who I was, which country I was from, what firm I worked at and how much money I made. She thanked me and gave me her precious gift because she felt I treated her well. Her genuine love touched me. She embraced me as a simple human being. I felt so small and naked in front of her. This made me think about the meaning and purpose again about my work.

IPO, Y2K and the Tech Bubble

Two years went by quickly. The two most significant events I experienced were the IPO of Goldman Sachs and Y2K. Everybody in Goldman Sachs was allocated shares before the IPO. After the IPO, when the share price rose, I realised it was a small fortune.

Y2K for an IT person was very special. Everyone in the IT department was nervous and excited at the same time when preparing for Y2K. Many projects were carried out to prevent any potential risks. Finally, we allocated seventy-two hours of rotation coverage during Y2K to monitor the IT system. It was like a big festival for me. With some minor issues, most of the system entered 1 January, 2000, without any problems. We were in a new century!

Since I joined Goldman Sachs in 1998, the technology bubble has kept growing and growing and the stock market has been rising and rising. Both the banking industry and the technology industry were enjoying a good time. More and more people from Goldman Sachs quit joining "dot com" companies. I heard stories that the entire banking team who served a technology company as a client went to join the company before the IPO and everybody made a fortune. Engineers from IT departments were also quitting left and right to start or join dot com companies. I got head-hunted several times to join technology start-ups but didn't understand their business models or know exactly what value they were creating. I didn't join any of them.

There was an internal job posting that caught my attention. The Private Wealth Management Department was hiring a technology banker who not only understood investment but also understood technology so that they could serve high-net-worth clients better investing in technology companies. That was my dream when I studied both business management and computer science. I always wanted to use technology to serve the business. Also, working as a banker at Goldman Sachs was always a dream. I applied and got into the interviews.

One million or one billion dollars?

One of the interviews was with a VP of PWM. He asked me: "Do you want to make one million or one billion dollars in ten years?" I was only twenty-seven at that time. To me, one million dollars sounded like much money. "I am more than happy with one million dollars!" I replied. "Great! This is the right place for you, then. I am forty-two. I made three point four million last year. If you work hard here, you could make one million dollars in ten years." "However," he added, "if you want to make one billion dollars, go and start your own company now. In ten years, please come back as our client." "No, no, no. I am happy with one million dollars in ten years. I promise I will work very hard."

I got the offer! I transitioned from an engineer to a technology banker within Goldman Sachs.

I had a new dream, a new goal. I had a fresh start! The VP became my new boss.

They again put me in a training programme in New York for three months. It was very similar to the last time. I met the brightest people from all around the world.

The most memorable moment was a speech by the Global Head of Sales of PWM. He was a tall, strong, handsome white guy in his forties. He looked like a football player turned movie star with perfect white teeth. Later I found that's exactly what happened. He played football at Harvard and studied at a drama school.

He started his speech with a story about himself.

"When I was at college, I worked at a home centre as a part-time job. My job was as a salesman to the customers who came to the home centre. I was confident I would be the top sales because the job seemed easy. I worked hard to remember the names and where the products were placed on the shelves. When customers came in the shop, I ran faster than anyone else to greet the customer and ask them what they needed. Then I ran to the shelves to get the products as quickly as possible, helped the customer to pay and ran to the next customer. I thought, using this strategy, I would be the number one sales in the home centre.

After one month, when the manager announced the ranking, I was number two. Close! I will work harder by remembering more products and running faster. I did exactly as I planned. I was still number two the following month. Who was number one? I checked. The number one salesman was an old guy who was not good-looking and couldn't run faster than me. How can he be number one? I wondered.

Let me work even harder next month and beat him. With the rivalry in mind, I always ensured I reached the customer faster than he did. I ran and ran to a point I couldn't work harder. I was sure I served more customers than he did. When the ranking was announced the following month, I was still number two and the old guy was still number one!

I surrendered. I walked over to him and asked: "How come you never ran as fast as I did and served fewer customers than me but made more sales?", "Let me tell you why," the old guy said. "You always asked what the customers wanted and just fetched them what they wanted as fast as you could." "Yes, isn't that what a salesman is supposed to do?" "You know what I asked the customers?" the old guy said. "I not only asked them what they needed but, more importantly, why they needed it." The old guy continued: "For example, a customer came to our shop and asked for a brush. Instead of running to get him a brush and sending him away as quickly as possible, I asked him why he needed it. He told me he needed the brush to paint his bathroom. Then I asked him many questions, such as, did you buy the water-proof paint? How old is your house? If your bathroom needed painting, what about the walls? Any problems with your water pipes? Then he told me, it was an old house. It had exactly the problems I said, but he wanted to start with the bathroom first. I told him I could go to your place and take a look. I could estimate all the places that needed to be fixed and give an estimate. If you buy everything from us, we could give you a discount. He was so happy someone could help him with everything he was not an expert at. It took me the whole day to serve one client. However, instead of selling him one brush, I sold him the solution to fix the entire house.

"So, to be the best sales, you don't just ask the customers what they need, but also ask them why they needed it.

You care about them by thinking from their point of view and giving them a solution. Not only can you make a lot more sales, but also you will gain a friend."

Wow! We were all looking at each other and amazed by the story.

"Later, I worked a part-time job at a fishing goods shop. A guy came into the shop and asked to buy a fishing rod. I asked him, 'What do you need it for? Are you an experienced fisherman?' He told me he had never fished before. He had been a successful but busy businessman and never spent time with his family. He knew his family loved the sea. He wanted to buy a fishing rod to spend time with his family fishing. 'You know, fishing can be tough if you have never done it before.' I told him. 'Yes, you are right. But what else can I do?' He shrugged. There was a boat docked outside the fishing shop. 'Can you sail?' I asked him. 'Yes, I used to sail when I was young.' 'Maybe it's better to sail with your family in a boat. You can do something you are good at. Your family is on the same boat with you on the sea. It's perfect for you to get close and have some conversation.' 'Yes, that'd be perfect!' He was excited. 'Let me ask the owner if the boat is for sale.' I asked the owner. He was looking to sell his boat. Finally, the man who came into our shop to buy a fishing rod ended up buying a boat and a fishing rod!"

A typical day at the PWM department

Life in PWM was very different from IT. The working hours were much longer and more intense. Also, unlike the international IT department, I was the only foreigner in the PWM department. Most of our high-net-worth clients were Japanese. We must have native-level Japanese capability to communicate with them. Also, unlike the casual atmosphere in the IT department, people in PWM were much more formal. Everyone wore suits every day. A tailor came into the office to make a suit for my boss one day. My boss called me to make a suit for myself as well. He told me that I needed some good-looking tailor-made suits to be a successful banker. He showed me his suits and shirts, all tailor-made with his name embroidered – the couple of suits he had just ordered each cost about five thousand dollars. I was amazed and asked him how many suits he had. "About fifty," he said. "How many shirts do you have?" I added. "I don't remember exactly, about three times the number of suits, I guess?" "One hundred and fifty?" I almost shouted. Why do you need so many suits and shirts? I wondered. Finally, I got myself measured and picked up the cheapest material, which cost about eight hundred dollars. I had my first tailor-made suit in gray and blue stripes. I ordered the pants with suspenders. Now I really looked like a Wall Street banker!

I decided to work one hundred hours a week to brush up on my financial skills and strengthen my understanding of technology companies' technologies and business models. I knew I wasn't the best IT person; I was far from a top private banker. However, combining those two skills, I aimed to be the best technology banker.

My typical day was like this. I woke up at 6am, Turned on the TV and started watching the stock market news. I got into the office at around 6:30am. Prepare for the morning meetings. At 7am, I went to the Equity trading floor to attend the morning meeting. I took notes about the closing of the New York Stock Exchange and thought about what happened there and what could be the implication for the Tokyo Stock Exchange that day. At 7:30, I went to the Fixed Income trading floor to join their morning meeting. I did the same by taking notes on the latest news about the bond market in New York and strategies for Japan market. There were four financial analysts in the PWM department. I was one of them. We returned to our department and shared our learning through a short debriefing meeting. One of us took turns to summarise a one-minute voice message. We called it daily market news. The person recorded the voice message into the voicemail system. Everybody in the PWM department could access and listen to the voice message system.

Some of the salespeople went directly to client meetings in the morning to listen to the voice message on the way. Most of the team members in the PWM department came to the office around 8:30. First thing in the morning, before the stock market opened at 9am, each team had an internal morning meeting to discuss the strategy for the day. Based on the market situation, the team members decided what financial products we recommended to buy or sell for the clients. After the meeting, the salespeople started calling the clients. The Financial Analysts oversaw trading among team members.

I started the trading software on my computer and started trading based on the orders we got from the salespeople. The trading hours of the Tokyo Stock Exchange were 9am to 3pm, with a one-hour break 11:30-12:30. Most of the time, I didn't have lunch. My adrenaline was high. I was like a car engine revved to the red zone for five hours.

While trading, I constantly communicated with the salespeople to report the status. Later, I directly talked to the clients on the phone to report the results. I needed to coordinate with the traders on the trading floor for big block trades. After the stock market closed at 3pm. I rushed downstairs to grab a sandwich. Eating at my desk, I was filing and completing the paperwork for the trades done for the day. At 5pm, the London Stock Exchange opened. Although only sometimes, we got some orders to execute there as well. Salespeople started to leave the office around 6pm to 8pm. Until then, I needed to update client portfolios and write emails and reports for client communication.

At around 8pm, I went downstairs to buy a bento box for dinner and breathed some fresh air. Between 8pm and 10pm, I could finally slow down a little bit. It was my favourite time of the day. I could read books or research reports to improve my understanding and knowledge of financial markets and products. I could research technology companies online and study their technologies and business models. The New York Stock Exchange opened at 10pm or 11pm Tokyo time, depending on daylight saving time. I started to trade again on the US stock market, either through the system myself or by coordinating with traders in New York. At around midnight, I finally got out of the office. Instead of returning home, I often drank at bars in Roppongi with other traders and bankers. When I finally got back home, it was about 2am. I took a quick shower and slept for three or four hours.

On the weekends, I continued to read analyst reports and books. There were always piles of reports on my desk and at home.

The PWM department had about thirty people and was divided into four teams. Each team had a team leader: Vice President, one or two Associates, one admin person and one Financial Analyst. All the VPs and Associates had MBA degrees. The Financial Analysts were college graduates. Each team managed twenty to fifty clients. I felt lucky because I was in a team with the most significant number of clients. Also, we have some very influential clients. We had twenty clients on the Forbes Top one hundred wealthiest people in Japan. To name a few, Mikitani-san was the founder and CEO of Rakuten, the largest Ecommerce platform in Japan. Mori family owned the largest real estate company in Japan. They owned so many buildings in the centre of Tokyo that they had to name them by numbers. Shigeta-san was the founder and chairman of Hikari Tsushin. He used to be the youngest CEO who went IPO in Japan. Yasuda-dan was the founder of the famous retail chain Don Quixote.

Big mistakes

The trading system was relatively simple. I input the stock ticker number, found the right stock and input the number of shares. There were many options to buy or sell with a set price or market price. There were two big buttons at the bottom of the screen. On the left was a green button that said Buy. On the right was a red button that said Sell. Although I had training for the trading system. There were only a few steps to operate and there were only two choices: buy or sell. I was still nervous because it was a lot of money exchanged once I triggered the button. The first time, my hands were shaking and sweating. I confirmed and reconfirmed the ticker number of the stocks, numbers and prices. Hitting the buy or sell button was the most nervous moment. The VP told me many times, don't make mistakes, confirm, confirm and confirm before hitting the button. He told me that people often hit the wrong button even though there were only two choices. At first, I thought, how could anyone make mistakes like that? It was so simple; there were only two choices, buy or sell. By paying attention, I would never make mistakes like that.

All the above operations must be executed promptly because the stock price keeps moving. If I did it slowly, I could cause loss for our clients.

The orders came as pieces of paper. Like the buttons' colours, the selling order sheet was pink and the buying order sheet was blue. The order sheets would pile up on my desk on a big day. My desk had two trays, one for buying order sheets and one for selling order sheets. After executing each order, I wrote down the share prices on the order sheets, punched two holes and filed them in a folder.

One day, I made the fatal mistake of hitting the wrong button. Instead of selling, I executed buying shares. After realising I had hit the wrong button, I felt my heart was about to burst. I ran to report to the VP. He immediately told me to quickly recover by selling double the number of shares. Fortunately, the share price rose during the period. Not only was there was no loss, but we also made a small profit. The team leader made me write a letter of reflection. He told me that I was lucky. If there was a loss occurred to recover the mistake, the amount must be paid from the commission of the team.

Unfortunately, during my two and half years at PWM, I made another mistake. The second time, I wasn't lucky. I incurred a loss to the team. I wrote a letter of reflection again. I felt so sorry for the team and ashamed of myself. However, the team leader was generous. He didn't blame me much. He told me to pay extra attention and not to do it a third time.

It's all about money

The salespeople were paid by the commission from the transactions of our clients. For example, no matter whether the client bought or sold financial products, Goldman Sachs charged a three per cent commission on the value of the transaction. Thirty per cent of the commission was paid as compensation to the salespeople and seventy per cent of the commission belonged to the company. The team leader told me that the salespeople of Goldman Sachs were like entrepreneurs who just used the signboard of Goldman Sachs but must create businesses by themselves. I did a calculation. For example, Mikitani-san had eight hundred million dollars of assets under management with our team. If we turned the assets around once a year, Goldman Sachs could earn three per cent of eight hundred million dollars, twenty-four million dollars. The salesperson got thirty per cent of that which was seven million two hundred thousand dollars! That's why private bankers on Wall Street were among the highest-paid bankers in the world.

I quickly realised there was a conflict of interest between clients and the company. Goldman Sachs always made money regardless of whether the clients made money or not. Since the salespeople made money on the commission of the transactions, they always had the motivation to have clients buy or sell their assets. The salespeople couldn't make any money if the clients didn't buy or sell. That was why the trend was that the private banking industry was moving from a commission-based to a fee-based structure. A fee-based structure would charge a fixed fee on the Asset Under Management of clients. To align the interest further, the fee was also performance-based. If the performance of a private banker beats the benchmark, for example, S&P500, by a certain percentage, the fee becomes higher and vice versa. The fee-based structure aligned interests between clients and the private banker; however, it meant it was harder for the private bankers to make money. Goldman Sachs still used a commission-based structure because this could attract more "wolf-like" private bankers and thus gather more assets quickly. The key to making money for the private bankers was not only increasing asset-under-management but also increasing the transaction volume of the asset.

Rules of the money game

However, making money as a private banker was not easy. My VP told me about the rules of the game.

The minimum requirement to open an account at Goldman Sachs PWM was twenty million dollars. The new associates who graduated from business schools and joined PWM had two years to accumulate eighty million dollars of Assets Under Management. Suppose the minimum requirement was unmet; the associate must leave the firm.

Since the number of wealthy individuals in Japan was limited, finding the target client became the key. In that regard, the private bankers competed with private bankers in other firms and within Goldman Sachs.

At the PWM department, we had a system to manage target clients. Every salesperson could only list a limited number of target clients in the system. The rule is that one client can only be approached by one salesperson at a time. Once a salesperson locks in a target client name, he has exclusivity to approach the client for six months. After six months, if the salesperson couldn't convert the target client to open an account with us, the target client was released from that salesperson. Other salespeople could lock in the target client and start approaching for six months. The release of target clients happened at midnight. It didn't happen every day, but when it happened, all the teams became rivals and fought to scramble the clients. One night, members of two teams stayed late in the office to scramble for a big client to be released at midnight. Everybody was watching the computer system and waiting for the turn of the clock.

When the clock turned midnight, they all clicked on the name. My team got it! The VP made a victory pose and looked at the other team. The other team members shook their heads and left the office. I felt it was thrilling but didn't feel good about the scene.

Rules were to be broken

At the PWM department, although my role was to trade and manage portfolios of clients, I always wanted to find potential clients as the salespeople did.

I was living on the top floor of a small three-storey apartment building. The first floor was a yakitori restaurant run by the owner of the building. I often ate there and chatted with the owner, who was the chef.

One day, when I was eating there, the landlord asked me: "You are a private banker at Goldman Sachs, right?" "Yes," I replied. "I have a friend who is a founder and CEO. His company just went public. His net worth was about six hundred and forty million. Maybe you guys can manage his asset," he said. "Really? Of course! Can you please make an introduction?" I felt I was so lucky.

I rushed to the office and checked the system. However, a salesperson on another team already locked in the CEO. I was disappointed and told my team leader about this situation. To my surprise, the VP told me to introduce him to the client. I asked him if that would be a violation of the rules. He told me it was fine. I connected my landlord with my team leader and didn't participate in the following meetings.

After a couple of months, one day, my team leader came back and called me to his room. He closed the door and whispered to me: "We got him! Thanks to your introduction, the CEO opened an account with us and deposited twenty million dollars!" I was so happy and was about to shout. He put his fingers over his mouth and said: "Don't tell the other team." I started to worry. "Are we violating the rules? What's going to happen?" "Don't worry; I will take care of it," my team leader said.

I came out of his office with mixed feelings of happiness and worry. I saw my team leader walk into the office of the managing director and close the door. I couldn't hear what they were talking about, but they both looked at me through the glass. They must be talking about my introduction to the client. Do I get the credit? I was anxious.

Soon they both walked out. The managing director shouted to everybody in the office: "Let's have a quick meeting, everybody. Let's go to the conference room." Everybody left their desks, entered the big conference room and stood there. The managing director stood in front of the crowd and spoke: "There was a violation of the Client Management system by Lu. He knew the other team already locked the client but still contacted the client. Thanks to his team leader for saving the situation. Since Lu is still new in our department, we will not punish him, but please make sure this won't happen again."

"What? Me? I violated the rule?" I couldn't believe my ears. Everybody stared at me with anger. I looked at my team leader. He quickly avoided eye contact with me and looked somewhere else. I felt deeply wronged by this accusation but couldn't say anything in front of people. I walked out of the conference room and sat at my desk; I felt powerless. Not only did I lose trust in my team leader, but also, I felt lost hope of becoming a successful private banker. If this is what it takes to make money, I rather not do it.

I was disillusioned and lost my motivation to work for weeks. I worked so hard to get here. I thought my dreams were coming true. I thought I was lucky. However, I didn't expect this to happen to me. I thought my team leader was a liar. I didn't want to work for him anymore. Finally, I decided to talk to my team leader. I walked into his office and closed the door. "I want to quit," I told him. "Why did you do something like that to me? Why did you make up a lie like that? I am going to tell the truth to the managing director and the other team." "Sorry," he said. "I was wrong. Please don't quit. But you need to know; this is the game." "What about I tell the truth to the managing director?" "No, let's talk to him together." I didn't trust what he would say behind the closed door. He agreed.

We walked into the office of the managing director. My team leader suggested I talk. I explained the whole situation to the managing director. The managing director looked at my team leader, shook his head and pointed his finger at him. "You!" My team leader shrugged his shoulder and said, "Sorry!" The managing director called for another meeting with everyone in the conference room. He announced the violation of the rule by my team leader. However, he said, we don't want to change the salesperson to avoid a negative impact on the client. My team would still manage the client's assets. However, all the commissions from that client would go to the other team for one year. After one year, the commission would be split fifty-fifty between two teams. After three years, the total commission would go to my team.

I felt relief. However, my energy couldn't become the same level as before. After a couple of months, another incident happened. The associate who targeted the same client that was taken away by us was fired. During the two years since he joined the firm, he only contracted sixty-five million dollars of assets. Not meeting the eighty-million-dollar threshold, he had to leave. I felt so bad because he could have stayed if I had introduced him to the client with the twenty-million dollar asset. I felt guilty for him.

One afternoon, as he was packing. I walked over to him and said sorry to him. I told him the story that I had the contact of that client, but my team leader made me give it to him. I wasn't strong enough to do the right thing. He said: "Don't worry; it's not your fault. Even if you gave me his contact, I may not have closed the deal. Your team leader was a better salesperson." Watching him leave the office, I felt a sense of relief but felt something was wrong.

Soon, with the mental pressure, heavy workload and lack of sleep and working out, my health started to deteriorate. I started to have gastritis. I felt my candle of life burning shorter and shorter. I knew this was not sustainable. I was trading my life with experience and knowledge in finance. I heard one of my peer analysts fainted twice at work and got carried to the ER. She came back in one month. She got carried to ER again. She lost the capability to work permanently. Mental stamina and toughness, I remember one of the managing directors stressed during our orientation. To survive in Goldman

Sachs, I learned those were the must. However, I was not too fond of moral challenges.

The epiphany moment

One event ultimately made me realise I didn't belong in the banking world.

One night, I stayed late at night again to execute a block trade worth about five million dollars for a client with a trader in New York. I was told to call the client when the deal was done, no matter how late. After handling the trade with the trader in New York, I waited in the office for the result. Many big-screen TVs were hanging on the wall. Usually, they display market news and information. That night, it was showing a documentary about Muhammad Yunus. His background, creativity and heart for helping Bangladesh's poor people intrigued me. I resonated with his experience and was inspired by his courage.

Dr. Yunus grew up in Bangladesh. After graduating from college, he went to the US and got his Ph.D. in economics. He stayed in the US as an associate professor. That could be a dream for many people. However, he returned to Bangladesh and started a microfinance company, Grameen Bank, which aimed to reduce poverty. Grameen Bank got millions of people out of poverty and changed their lives. The documentary showed how fifty dollars could change a person's life. A Bangladesh woman used the fifty dollars to buy a cow to cultivate the field. Other women bought some bamboo to make baskets. The fifty dollars allowed them to learn skills and acquire tools and materials to make a living.

The trade was done. I got the report from the trader in New York. I called the client to give him a report that he just made five million dollars. I heard he was in a karaoke bar. It was noisy. There was the voice of girls singing and shouting. "Ok, got it." He briefly cut me off while I was reporting the detailed share prices. "That ice cream is mine!" He shouted to someone on the other side of the phone and hanged.

In front of me, the TV screen showed the happy faces of the poor Bangladesh women whose lives were changed by fifty dollars. The noise of the Karaoke bar from the phone still echoed in the air. I stood up and tears broke out from my eyes. I thought about my family having to borrow money to send me to Japan. I thought about myself washing dishes and eating the leftover food from the garbage bin in a restaurant. Our lives were like the people in Bangladesh. There were even poorer people in China than us.

Now, what am I doing? I just made a rich man richer. He got five million dollars richer and spent that money in the Karaoke bar, drinking expensive champagne and partying with girls. The five million dollars didn't impact him or the world much. With that amount of money, how many lives could be changed?

I felt like a parasite, earning a living from the commission made by making the rich man richer. Compared to Dr Yunus, I felt I was so small. What am I doing with my time and talent? I asked myself. Shall I spend my life and talent making rich people richer or helping poor people to change their lives?

At that moment, I finally understood why I felt something was wrong in my life. I felt the calling to use my talent to create businesses that benefit many, not the wealthiest. However, I always had a dream to get an MBA from the top schools in the US. I set goals to leave Goldman Sachs, earn an MBA and start a social business.

Chapter 8
Road to Stanford

You can do it!

Once the goals were set, I started working hard toward them. First, I needed to decide which business school to go to. At the same time, I must get a high GMAT score to get into the top business schools. Also, I needed to prepare the essays for each business school I applied to.

I enrolled in an MBA preparation school in Japan and bought many books for GMAT and essay writing. Anticipating the work and hours needed for MBA preparation, I decided to quit my job and focus.

I walked into my team leader's office one day and told him I quit because I needed to prepare for business school. My team leader got angry and spoke: "How could you be so irresponsible? You can't just quit like this. You must give us a few months to find someone to replace you." He added: "When I prepared for business school, I didn't quit working. I was working while preparing!" He took me to the managing director's office.

"Great to hear you are applying for business school?" the managing director said. "I can write you a recommendation letter to Harvard." The managing director had a completely different reaction to my team leader. "I know you are the best. You can go to the best business schools." The managing director continued: "However, you don't need to quit. You can work and prepare for business school at the same time." He tapped my shoulder and said: "You can do it!"

Got out of the managing director's office and I felt good. "He thinks I can go to Harvard! And he is going to write me a recommendation letter!" After a while, I figured he basically said the same thing as the team leader but packaged it differently. What excellent communication skills! I felt I had learned something new. If they could do it, I could do it too. I decided to work harder and prepare for business school simultaneously.

I still worked for sixteen hours a day. After going home at night, I studied GMAT. The only time I could squeeze was sleeping.

The ranking list

I researched the rankings from various media about business schools, such as the Wall Street Journal, The US News, the Financial Times, etc. Each media ranked differently; for example, some ranked Harvard number one. Some ranked Stanford number one. Some ranked Wharton number one. Each media had its criteria and value for ranking. However, the names among the top ten were similar. Two years of time and money in business school were a considerable investment for me. I decided to research the top ten business schools myself and develop my own ranking. I felt that business school selection was subjective, just like finding a girlfriend. A happy relationship comes from subjective value alignment, not from external specs or ranking by someone else. I must choose the school that I like. I must visit the top 10 business schools and create my own criteria based on my own experience.

I used all my paid vacation days to travel to the US and visit top-ranking business schools. The names on my list were Harvard, MIT, Columbia, Dartmouth, Yale, Wharton, Babson, Kellogg, Stanford, Berkeley, UCLA and USC. However, the two names, Harvard and Stanford, were at the top among all the other schools. I showed my list to the managing director. He said: "Just apply to Harvard. Forget about Stanford. Harvard had a fourteen per cent acceptance rate, double the seven per cent of Stanford. Furthermore, I am from HBS. I can write you a recommendation letter."

I created my own ranking criteria based on what I thought was important. The most important factor for me was the business school's student body. First, I could learn the most from the students instead of the professors and books. The students at the top business schools were from different industries around the world. I could only meet them there in the business schools, whereas I could learn from the famous professors by taking online courses or reading their books.

Second, when people talked about the number one gain out of business schools, it was always the connection with the alumni network. It was more about the quality other than the quantity of the network. Even if you have access to a vast alumni database but no one wants to help you, what's the difference between the alumni database and a phone book? I thought the depth of the relationship was more important than the number of people you know. For big schools with close to one thousand students per year, it's hard to remember all the names of your classmates, not to mention build a deep relationship with a great number of people. I gave smaller schools higher scores than big schools.

I also gave more weight to entrepreneurship because I knew I wanted to start a business that benefits people. That was why Babson was on the list. It was ranked high in terms of entrepreneurship.

Environment, both physical and the local community, was also important to me. I understood human was the product of the environment. The environment was something I must feel with my body by being there rather than getting second-hand information from online or books.

Before I went, I already knew Stanford was at the top of my ranking because it ticked all the boxes that I thought were important. More importantly, it had a course called Social Entrepreneurship which I longed for after watching the documentary about Dr Yunus.

The road trips

I packed the school visits into two trips, because most of the schools on my list were on the East and West coasts, while only Kellogg was in the middle of the US.

On the first trip, I went to the East coast. My number one school on the East coast was Harvard. Not only was it in the top three all the time and everybody knew it, but also my managing director graduated from both Harvard university and the felt business school.

The moment I stepped on the campus, I felt the noble atmosphere of Harvard. The New England-style buildings were elegant and solemn. The red bricks and white frames of the windows made me feel I need to wear an oxford shirt, a preppy vest and a navy blazer to match the style. Watching the students on the campus, I could feel their intelligence and pride.

I randomly talked to the students in the cafeteria and introduced myself as a prospective student. Some said they were busy. A couple of students invited me to attend their classes. "No problem, just sit in the back" they said. I followed them to the classroom.

The "Strip show"

Sitting in the classroom, I was watching the students around me. I tried to imagine myself sitting in the classroom. However, I forgot what class it was because what happened at the end of the class was so shocking that I couldn't forget.

After the professor left the room, a couple of students went to the front of the class. They announced it was the last class of the semester and called some names. There were three students called to go to the front of the classroom.

Suddenly, the room became dark, only with a few lights on like spotlights, irradiating the podium. At the same time, dance music started. The three students whose names were called got on the podium and started dancing, "What's going on?" I wondered.

The next moment, they started to strip their clothes off. Everybody in the classroom started to whistle and shout. The classroom was turning into a strip dance club. I was intrigued to see such an odd scene. Fortunately, they didn't strip to the last pieces of their clothes. A few minutes later, they got off the podium. They grabbed their clothes and backpacks. They waved their hands and left the classroom. Students started to leave the classroom as well. I followed the crowd and asked the student who invited me: "What was that?" "They are out," he said. "They were in the bottom five per cent of the class this semester. It's a tradition that the last five per cent of the class will do a strip dance in front of the class," the student answered and walked away. I stood there, shocked and couldn't move. I didn't want to be one of the three students stripping on the podium.

Falling in love at first sight

After Harvard, I visited MIT, Wharton, Columbia, Babson, Dartmouth and Yale. I did the same as I did at Harvard. I randomly picked students to talk to and followed them to their classes. The friendliness of the students and whether they loved their experience were the most important criteria to me. If the students were friendly to prospective students, they could treat their classmates equally. If they loved their experiences at the school, they could treat other alumni well and contribute to the school's network.

For some reason, I couldn't picture myself at MIT, Babson and Dartmouth. At Wharton and Columbia, I met students who said they hated the school. Yale was the friendliest school among all the business schools on the East Coast. Every student I met was friendly; they even called their Chinese classmates to meet me and talk about their experiences as foreign students at Yale. It was a small school with about two hundred and fifty students. I felt they were like a family.

On my second trip, I visited Kellogg, Stanford, Berkeley, UCLA and USC. The only reason Kellogg was on my list was that my favourite marketing guru Philip Kotler taught at Kellogg. I had a chance to meet him when I was helping my professor organise a global marketing event in Japan. I liked Kellogg. The students were friendly. However, the weather was so cold during the winter when I visited. I remember I had to go through underground tunnels between buildings. I got a terrible cold and had a fever for a few days. I soon got recovered when I landed in California.

Fumi, my dorm mate at Saitama University, was a graduate student at UCSF then. He showed me around San Francisco. The following day, I took the train to Stanford. Unlike San Francisco, which was always foggy and cold, Palo Alto was sunny and warm. When the train stopped at the Palo Alto station, I walked out of the train and saw the morning dew shining on the green meadow. The air smelled fresh and crisp, even a little bit sweet.

I took a deep breath and walked toward the campus of Stanford through the beautiful Palm Drive. Unlike the schools on the East Coast, Stanford had no tall buildings. All the buildings were low and widely spread. The orange-coloured roof tiles and beige-coloured walls created a great contrast with the blue sky. The sky looked more extensive and open than any school I had visited.

The students' attitudes were like the sky as well. They wore T-shirts, short pants, sunglasses and flip-flops. Skateboards and yoga mats were everyday items alongside their backpacks. I felt they were outdoor adventurers or surfers rather than the elite preppies on the East Coast. The students were relaxed and friendly. Nobody treated me like a stranger. I felt at home at Stanford. I felt excited but with a little bit of nervousness. I almost felt like I had visited a dream house but couldn't afford it.

I visited Berkeley, UCLA and USC. The students were all friendly. They all loved their schools. However, after visiting all the schools, Stanford stood as number one in my heart. It felt like falling in love at first sight with a girl. She was so beautiful and stood out among all the girls. Every man was chasing her. How could I date her? Why did she choose me? Stanford was the most competitive business school to get into in the world. My heart was beating when I thought about it.

After I finished my trips to the business schools, I put together my own ranking. Stanford was number one, Yale was number two. Harvard was number three. Berkeley and UCLA were number four and five. The rest of the ranking was not necessary to me. I couldn't picture myself in any of those schools.

Cramming the GMAT

Next, I needed at least six hundred scores for the GMAT exam to get into those top business schools. Although there were GMAT exams every day, one can only take the test once per month. One could take as many GMAT exams as possible, but only the last four scores were recorded for application. Once you take the fifth test, the first test score disappears. The GMAT exam was computer-based. The score showed up on the screen right after the test.

There were three rounds of application deadlines for business schools. However, the largest pool of admission was from the second round. The deadlines for second-round applications were mostly around December or January.

It was September; I had four chances for the GMAT exam before the application deadline in December. I planned the test dates to be the last available date of the month to give me the most time to prepare.

My September test score was five hundred and eighty. Not too bad for the first time. I continued studying hard for a month and went to the test centre in late October 2001. During the test, I felt the test was easy. It was a bad sign because GMAT was a Computer Adaptive Test (CAT). A computer entirely generated the test questions, one question at a time. Each time I entered an answer, the CAT evaluated my response and determined my next question's difficulty level. If I answered the question correctly, the next question would become more complex and vice versa. After completing the questions, I clicked the button to show the score. Four hundred and sixty! I was shocked. I didn't expect my scores to be this bad. Two more chances! I decided to study even harder.

I bought more GMAT practice exam books and worked on them every night after I got home. I only slept a few hours per night. I continued one hundred hours' work per week and added the GMAT study on top of it. I felt my body and brain were burning out.

The GMAT books were piled on the ground to be more than a metre high in my room. I took the GMAT exam for the third time in late November. My score rose a bit to five hundred and ten. Although far from my target to be over six hundred, I was encouraged by the improvement and determined to try my best for the final exam in December.

Bad and good news

The tragic accident of 9/11 happened only a couple of months ago. I was sad to see the Twin Towers collapse on TV. I still remember my two-week training on the top floors of Windows on the World. Fortunately, none of my colleagues and friends died in the accident. The financial market crashed after that. However, nothing could change my decision to attend a US business school.

One Sunday in December, I got a "To All" email from the managing director that everyone must go to the office on Monday at 8am. The Legal Department was also copied in the email. I had a bad feeling.

Monday, we gathered in the big conference room of the PWM department. The managing director and two people from Legal Department were sitting in the front. The managing director announced a piece of shocking news. The company had decided to shut down the PWM department – twenty-five out of thirty people would be laid off. The remaining five people would be transferred to other departments. The secretary of my team leader started to cry. I looked at the associate in my team. His face turned dark. His wife just got hospitalised and his son was only two months old. We were told to wait at our desk and wait for individual communication about the severance packages.

I went back to my desk. My computer was logged off. I couldn't log on anymore. I started gathering my stuff in a cardboard box. This happened so suddenly. However, I thought I was lucky. "Great, now I have more time to prepare for the GMAT exam and MBA application." I got a severance package of six months' salary. Adding my savings, I could afford to pay for the tuition of an MBA.

Cracking the essays

Another massive task for the MBA application was writing essays. Each business school had a different set of questions for essays. I chose the ones from Harvard as a base because the questions of other schools were similar, such as, "What are your career goals?", "What are your strengths and weaknesses?", "Describe your best failure." etc. Also, there were limits to the number of words for the questions. However, there was only one question from Stanford and there was no limit to the number of words. "What matters to you the most and why?" was the question.

I had been writing essays for other business schools. They were relatively easy because they were like typical interview questions. There were also many templates on how to answer those questions. I finished writing essays for all the business schools except Stanford. I found it hard to write because the topic was too deep and vague. I hired a consultant Dayton who specialised in business school essay writing.

Dayton told me that the key to the essay was to be true to myself. There was no need to guess what the admission officers wanted to see but to reveal the true and unique self. The best essay was that no matter what paragraph was picked, the reader could quickly figure out it was uniquely from me.

What matters most and why? This question was so profound that I had to search the deepest part of my heart and memory. It was a question about my value system and why I formed my unique value system. The value system was my identity. I started thinking deeply about who I was, where I came from and why I did things I did in my life. It took me three months to write this essay. There was no template I could copy from. I spent much time reflecting on my life. I sat down with my best friends and asked them what they thought about me that was unique and why. I wrote, scrapped, re-wrote and scrapped. I wrote about ten versions and still wasn't satisfied with my writing. This question was always on my mind when working, eating and sleeping. Finally, I decided to be honest with myself. I wrote about stories in my life, from the push-ups in middle school to playing in the basketball team, from changing from fashion design to selling computer magazines, from leaving China to coming to Japan, from washing dishes to getting all As in Saitama University, from founding Try Me to private banking at Goldman Sachs.

I also wrote that I wanted to build social enterprises to use my business skills to change millions of underprivileged people's lives. It was like a mini version of this book. I wrote about what I did, why I did it in the past and where I was heading. It turned out to be thirty pages. I showed it to Dayton. Dayton loved it and helped me with some wording in English. He told me: "This is it!"

I felt it was a love letter to my dream girl. It was about the true me, where I came from and where I was heading. Most importantly, why I needed her to complete my life. I told myself: "Even if you don't love me by reading this letter, I am happy too because that means I am not for you."

The last chance

No need to work anymore, I started to study full-time every day for my final trial of the GMAT on 30 December. I studied day and night. I exhausted all the books I could buy in Japan. I had my family buy GMAT books and CDs from China and mail them to me.

The deadline for the second-round application for Stanford was 4 January. I needed a GMAT score of over six hundred because I had already completed the essay.

I was nervous during the test. I had done enough training. I just needed to deliver it, I told myself. The four-hour exam went by quickly. After clicking the button, the result showed on the screen, Four hundred and eighty! What? My heart was about to explode. It was hurting. I couldn't believe my eyes. How could this be possible? I worked harder than last month and my score was even lower.

I felt so disappointed. I felt my dreams just broke. My dream girl just faded away. I lost the motivation to do anything. I went to a nightclub and decided to get drunk. For the past year, since I started preparing for my MBA application, I lived a disciplined life like a monk. I worked and studied sixteen hours a day. I didn't rest for the weekends. I didn't go out with my friends. My room was piled with GMAT books. However, all my hard work was ruined because of the GMAT score. I knew that with my highest score, five hundred and eighty, getting into any top business school was impossible. I kept drinking and drinking. I didn't want to think about the reality and the next steps. I woke up the next morning with a headache and did nothing for three days. On 2 January, for the first time in a year, I rented a video to watch at home. It was the movie The Truman Show. I resonated so much with the actor that I cried when I saw him struggle in the storm to search for his true love. I felt like I suddenly woke up. I put a big banner on the wall and wrote: "Never, Never, Never Give Up!!"

I looked up the GMAT online reservation system. The first available date was 4 January. It was the same day as the deadline for the application to Stanford. However, due to the time zone difference, I still had time to take the GMAT exam and submit the application online in time. I knew that my highest score was my first one, five hundred and eighty. If I retook the next GMAT exam, the five hundred and eighty scores would disappear from my record. If my score tomorrow were lower than five hundred and eighty, I would lose more opportunities even to get into second-tier business schools. However, without hesitation, I quickly reserved the date for the afternoon GMAT exam on 4 January. "Even with a one per cent possibility, I will try with one hundred per cent effort. Never, never, never give up!" I kept telling myself.

I had less than twenty-four hours to prepare before the exam. I had been drunk for the past three days and had done nothing. I had a headache and was in bad shape.

I walked into the testing centre and still had a headache. However, I sat down in front of the computer and was determined to squeeze all my intellectual power. The exam was difficult. Four hours never felt so long. I gritted my teeth, focused on every question and kept proceeding. Finally, the exam was over. My fate was one click away. I took a deep breath and clicked the "Show result" button.

640! Once I saw the score, I jumped and shouted 'Yes!". I felt it was a miracle!

I rode my bicycle home. The wind was blowing through my hair; I felt the wind of freedom and opportunity. I recalled all the days and nights I studied. I recalled how I almost lost hope, drunk for three days, but finally decided not to give up and bet on my last opportunity. I looked up at the sky and felt God was watching me. I laughed and cried at the same time. My chest became wet from my tears.

I rushed home, got on my computer and submitted my application to Stanford with a GMAT score six hundred and forty. I was exhausted. I felt like I had just finished a marathon. I did my best. I did all I could. I had no job. I had no back-up plan. Now it was time to wait and pray.

In the coming months, I got rejection letters from Wharton and Harvard. I got an admission from Babson. I didn't feel much disappointment or excitement. I knew I was waiting for my true love, Stanford.

One afternoon in April, a thick envelope arrived in my mailbox. It had a Stanford logo on it. I had a feeling of what it was. I opened it: "Congratulations on the admission to the Stanford Graduate School of Business." It was the happiest moment of my life. I felt like my dream girl had said yes to my proposal. I could see the blue sky of California. I could see the orange roofs and green meadows of the beautiful campus of Stanford. I called my grandmother and father and told them the good news. It was not just my dream come true. It was the dreams of my family that came true. After ten years in Japan, from washing dishes to entering Saitama University to entering Goldman Sachs, I finally had a chance to study at Stanford, one of the top business schools in the world. I felt I had not only survived but also thrived. I could only do this because of the values and the mindset I formed through my childhood with my family's influence.

Chapter 9
Transformational Experiences At Stanford

No label of others, no label of yourself

I was a little nervous on the orientation day at Stanford Graduate School of Business. I didn't know who my classmates were and thought seeing so many brilliant students from all industries and worldwide might be overwhelming.

However, when I got my name tag at the reception, I was told there were two rules to introduce myself. First, I couldn't say which country I was from. Second, I couldn't say which company or industry I used to work for. The purpose of the rule was to avoid labelling each other with prejudice. At first, I felt awkward when I started greeting other students. I remembered that "I am Chinese" was my starting phrase when interviewed in Japan. "I work at Goldman Sachs" was my first introduction line. However, it was refreshing to introduce myself without identifying my nationality and my career was so challenging. I didn't know what to say after "Hi, I am Lu." I was not alone. Other students felt awkward as well. We all smiled at each other and tried to start a conversation. I felt like I was in kindergarten, trying to learn how to speak and walk; however, after a while, we all got used to talking about our favourite vacations, sport, music and art. Our conversation became fun.

As we were talking, a gentleman walked in and introduced himself as the Admission Officer. His name was Derrick Bolton. When he started to shake hands with each of us, he looked at our name tags and started to say a line in our essays. When he shook my hand, he said, "Hi, Lu. Great to finally see you! You are the guy who washed dishes in Japan, right?" "Yes, but how could you remember all our stories?" I asked amazed. "I enjoyed them. I got the best job!" He winked at me and walked to the next student. We were all in awe of his memory and returned to our conversations. The first day, I was already impressed.

The NDA

On the first day of school, we found a sheet of yellow paper in each of the mailboxes of the first-year students. It was from the second-year students. It was a Non-Disclosure Agreement (NDA) of our GPA. GPA is an acronym for Grade Point Average. It is a number calculated from one's grades at a US university. The letter said that it was a tradition passed from previous classes. The current second-year students also got the same letter when they started the first day of school.

The letter stated that the NDA was from the students voluntarily rather than from the school. The school respects the students' freedom to adopt such agreements among themselves.

The agreement stated that although the students get GPAs from the school, we agreed not to disclose our

GPAs to anyone else. This included other students, parents and future employers.

Most of the letter explained the reason why such an agreement was proposed. It said that the purpose of the NDA was to foster and strengthen the culture of taking risks and helping each other. The goals of studying at Stanford GSB were not to gain as high as possible GPAs personally but to take risks, do something new and help each other succeed.

If the goal for students was to achieve the highest GPA possible, then everybody would choose courses in their vital areas and avoid weak areas. For example, a former banker would choose corporate finance and would not choose courses in areas he had never done before, such as organisational behaviour.

Similarly, if the goal was to achieve the highest GPA personally, the ex-banker student would be less likely to be motivated to help an ex-pianist classmate on corporate finance the night before the exam. Focusing on GPA could lead students to behave selfishly and compete with each other.

The agreement's purpose was to encourage us to go out of our comfort zone to challenge ourselves and help others succeed.

I was amazed. Not only did I resonate with Stanford's culture of helping each other rather than compelling with each other, but I was also touched by the students' courage and action to enforce such a culture. I remembered the public humiliation at Harvard Business School. What a big difference. People are products of the environment. Imagine how the students would behave differently after spending two years in those different environments. What would those people do in different companies after graduation from each school? I felt I loved Stanford even more.

Go out of my comfort zone

I decided to go out of my comfort zone and challenge myself to do things differently. First, I felt it was comfortable to hang out with Asian students and speak Chinese or Japanese. I decided I would spend more time with students from other countries. Second, it was comfortable for me to relate to students from investment banking and consulting backgrounds. I tried to talk to students from other industries.

One of the most important reasons for me to apply to Stanford was its strength in Social Entrepreneurship.

The founder of Rubicon, Rick Aubry, led us through a course for the whole semester. He invited different social entrepreneurs to talk about their stories each time. It was an eye-opening experience. I also participated in a social entrepreneurship project with engineering school students.

Stanford had a great engineering school. HP, Sun Microsystem, Google and many technology companies were born at Stanford. The project was to solve social problems by applying technologies and creating sustainable business models. One of the coaches was the founder of a social enterprise that brought electric generators and LED lights into homes not connected to the power grid. My project team's theme was to develop a low-cost way to deliver hearing-aid devices to low-income people.

As the businessperson in the team, I researched the cost structure of hearing-aid devices and studied the market landscape and insurance policies for such products. The key to social entrepreneurship was to do good and do well simultaneously. We needed to be creative to make a social impact and profit at the same time. I was encouraged by seeing so many successful examples that it was possible to do it.

I also decided to do something unique at Stanford. Stanford is in the centre of Silicon Valley. There are a lot of organisations and communities in the area. The ones I was interested in participating in were China business-related and technology startups. I met many people who later became famous founders and CEOs of technology start-ups in China and the US.

Napa was famous for the new world wines and was near Stanford. Fortunately, Stanford offered a wine-tasting class that counted one credit toward graduation. It was the last class on Friday afternoon. Not only did I learn a lot about wines, but I also had a great time making friends who were wine lovers.

I also enrolled in a sailing class at Stanford. I always wanted to learn to sail ever since I watched The Truman Show. This dream came true as well. I learned to sail a dinghy in the bay that Stanford owned. What an excellent way of spending a sunny Californian afternoon sailing in the San Francisco Bay!

Stanford's drama school was also famous. It was next to the Business School. I enrolled in a comedy class because I remembered the global head of sales in PWM at Goldman Sachs went to a drama school. I learned how to break the barriers of myself to play someone else and move my body and express emotion creatively.

There were other classes I wanted to go to but didn't have time, such as horseback riding and golf. Stanford had probably the best golf courses among all universities in the US. In the driving range, a big S sign in the distance showed where Tiger Woods hit.

Of course, the main courses at the Business School were rigorous. People may think that students don't study much in American universities. I can surely tell you that was not the case at Stanford. The content of the classes was challenging.

During class, we must concentrate and always try to answer the professors' questions correctly and make meaningful comments. Twenty per cent of the GPA was from class participation. The amount of work before and after classes was heavy. Not only had I to read the cases and textbooks, but also, I had to complete homework. Often, I needed to read more than one hundred pages of books between classes. Even though we signed an NDA, everybody was still working hard. I thought I could rest at the business school, but I was wrong. I felt I studied almost as hard as when I worked at Goldman Sachs.

Too many choices in life? Do what you remember in ten years

Working hard and playing hard was also a culture at Stanford. Every night multiple parties were going on. I felt twenty-four hours were not enough. Even if I had four or five bodies, I still couldn't have done all I wanted to do. Every day after school, I could choose to work out, study with my small team, attend student parties, or attend an event in Silicon Valley. I had to learn how to prioritise.

Whenever I was confused with choices, I always thought about which choice I would remember ten years from then. For example, I could prepare for the corporate finance exam the next day, attend a student dinner party, or join a Silicon Valley technology start-up gathering. I chose the party because I knew I wouldn't remember the corporate finance exam; I wouldn't remember the new faces among the Silicon Valley start-ups. Still, I could have the opportunity to get to know one of my classmates deeper and deepen our relationship, which could last for more than ten years.

People say that a business's success is about who you know and who knows you. I agree, but I think it's more about quality than quantity. I preferred smaller parties to the big ones where everyone had a short conversation and moved on to the next.

To get to know people deeper, I decided to host my own dinner party. Every Wednesday night, I invited five people from my class to my dorm. I cooked Chinese food for them and we had fun conversations. They called it Lu's dinner. Every week, my classmates wondered who would be invited. I decided to get to know one hundred classmates really well. After almost twenty years, some classmates still remembered Lu's dinner.

Two of my favourite classes that are still valid after twenty years

Other than Social Entrepreneurship, I also liked two other classes. I still remember them now.

One is Interpersonal Dynamics. We gave it a nickname, Touchy Feely. Because we all signed NDA, what happened in that class stayed in that class. I can't disclose the detail. However, I can tell what I learned. The class was designed to help people better understand their relationship with themselves and others. The class was based on the theory of the Johari Window. (Please see the picture below)

Johari Window

	Known to self	Not known to self
Known to others	Arena	Blind Spot
Not Known to Others	Façade	Unknown

Charles Handy calls this concept the Johari House with four rooms. Room one is the part of ourselves that we and others see. Room two contains aspects that others see but we are unaware of. Room three is the private space we know but hide from others. Room four is the unconscious part of us that neither ourselves nor others see.

The goals were the expansion of the Open (Arena) square at the expense of both the Unknown square and the Blind Spot square, resulting in greater knowledge of oneself, while voluntary disclosure of Private (Hidden or Facade) squares may result in greater interpersonal intimacy and friendship.

During the class, we laughed, cried, hugged, argued and eventually discovered a lot about ourselves and each other. We formed a much deeper relationship than before. Even today, when I solve conflicts with people, I still use the framework of touchy-feely. Some said business success was ten per cent IQ and ninety per cent EQ. I totally agree. Personal success could rely on IQ. However, in business, nobody can work alone. It's not only about how smart you are but also about gaining understanding and support from others. Touchy-feely never got outdated.

The other class was Creativity in Business. In the first class, the professor asked us: "How many of you were not passionate about your work but had to do it because it paid well and you used the money to do things you love?" Many students, including me raised their hands. "Then you are torn between making money by doing things you don't like and squeezing the rest of the time to do the things you love." "You only live once; why not do what you love and make money simultaneously?"

After the first class, the professor gave us the best homework I had ever had: "Do whatever you can to make next week the best week in your life. Write it down and report to us." After hearing the announcement, we were all excited. "Can I do anything?" one student asked. "Yes, ANYTHING! As long as it's legal and not negatively impacting others," the professor replied.

I listed everything I loved: surfing in Santa Cruz, listening to my favourite music while running on the beautiful campus at Stanford, eating at my favourite restaurant with my best friends and driving to Half Moon Bay to watch the sunset…

I tried hard to make every day the best. I was busy but excited. I tried not to do anything I disliked.

A week went by quickly. We gathered in the classroom again. I could feel the class was full of energy. When the professor asked the students one by one to report how they spent their week, everybody spoke confidently. The classroom was full of laughter.

"Congratulations!" he concluded. "You just made yourself the best week of your life. It was not given by anybody else. If you could do it last week, why don't you keep doing it next week? Why don't you do it for fifty-two weeks, a whole year? Why don't you do it for the rest of your life and make all the weeks of the rest of your life the best?"

Wow, I had a revelation. I had the responsibility and the capability to make my life the best. Nobody could stop me from making my life the best.

After that, the professor asked us: "What was the essence of the things you did to make you feel that you had the best time?" and how to apply the essence to work. He gave us an example: "If you love riding a motorcycle, the essence could be that you love the feeling of speed. However, you don't have to work as a professional motorcycle driver to enjoy the feeling of speed; you can recreate the feeling of speed by doing other things, for example, trading stocks. Then you can feel great and make money at the same time."

"Go and find a company that gives you the best feelings and makes the most money. If you can't find a company like that, create one yourself! In the following classes, we are going to learn how."

I was amazed by this concept. It was very similar to the Hedgehog Concept by Jim Collins.

The Hedgehog Concept is developed in the book Good to Great. A simple, crystalline concept that flows from a deep understanding of the intersection of three circles: 1) what you are deeply passionate about; 2) what you can be the best in the world at; and 3) what best drives your economic or resource engine.

Transformations from good to great come about by a series of good decisions made consistently with a Hedgehog Concept, supremely well executed, accumulating one upon another over a long period of time.

https://www.jimcollins.com/concepts/the-hedgehog-concept.html

Three Circles of the Hedgehog Concept

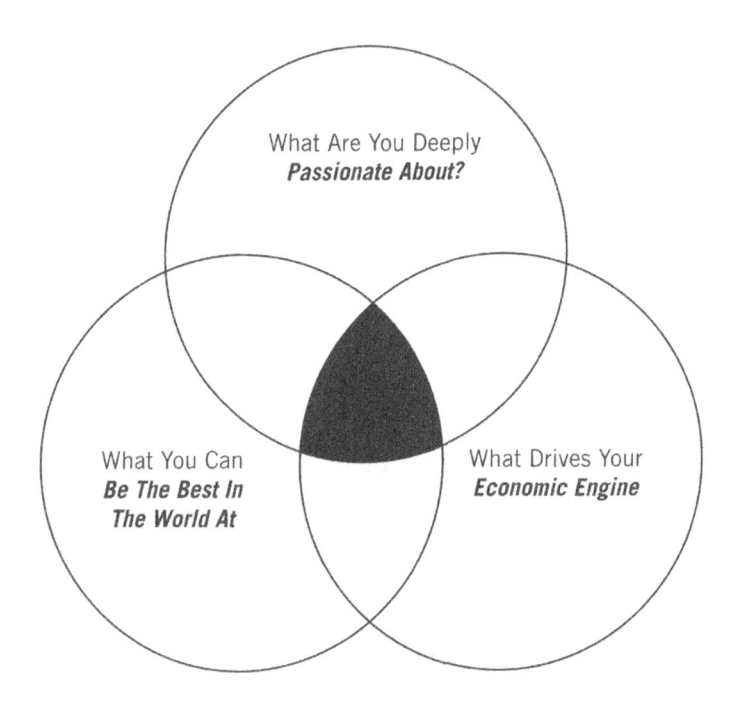

- What Are You Deeply *Passionate About?*
- What You Can *Be The Best In The World At*
- What Drives Your *Economic Engine*

After graduation, I used the inspiration from Creativity in Business and the framework of the Hedgehog Concept to start three of my businesses.

People are the products of the environment

After spending a year at Stanford, I started to understand why it was the incubator of entrepreneurs. It was the people at Stanford and Silicon Valley that made me feel that not only was entrepreneurship the coolest thing but also that I could do it. I felt unknown confidence that I could do it after meeting many entrepreneurs.

Steve Jobs came to speak to the students in the business school. This was his second time speaking at the Stanford Graduate School of Business. The first time, he met his wife. I was expecting him to speak like other big company CEOs about vision, mission, strategy, or some macro trend in the industry. However, he spent one entire hour talking about the new iPod. I could feel he was genuinely in love with that iPod. He told us how small it was, how cool it was and how revolutionary it was. He was like a big boy showing off his favourite toy to others. I felt his emotion was so pure and true. After his speech, I went to talk to him. I said: "What about selling this iPod to China?" Steve answered: "Good idea!" In a good way, I felt he was just a regular guy like me. He was more of a product manager than a CEO.

I also met Jeff Bezos in a class called Entrepreneurship and VC. Jeff was a guest speaker. After the class, I asked him: "Do you want to bring Amazon to China?" "We are thinking about it," he answered. Three years later, we met again in Beijing on the TV show Dialog by CCTV. I was representing the eCommerce start-ups in China. Jeff saw me and said: "I know you! What are you doing now?" I told him I had started an online shirt tailoring company. "Can you make me some shirts?" Jeff asked. "Sure, we have a campaign of buy ten get two free," I answered. "What about I buy ten and get three free?" he said. "What a great merchant; he always bargains," I thought. "Sure, a special deal for the most successful eCommerce CEO in the world!" I measured him, made thirteen shirts for him and sent them to the US. After a few weeks, I got a package from the US. It was a shirt sent by Jeff Bezos. He wrote the following on the shirt with his signature: "Please hold this shirt and ring the bell at Nasdaq! – Jeff Bezos"

Eric Schmidt, the then CEO of Google, was not only a guest speaker; he taught us for the entire semester. I asked him, with my signature question again: "Do you want to bring Google to China?" "Why not? I need you guys to tell me how to do it," he answered.

There were more speakers, such as the co-founders of Sun Microsystem, Scott McNealy and Vinod Khosla. I was amazed by their stories of being classmates at Stanford GSB and co-founding Sun Microsystems. Hearing these stories repeatedly, I felt everybody at Stanford thought it was possible to start a company with their classmates.

The topics of conversation among students were utterly different from colleagues at Goldman Sachs. Nobody talked about Wall Street or the stock market. The most exciting conversations were about new business models or someone who discovered a cool start-up with only three people but a technology that could change the world.

The summer internship searching season began in the middle of the first year. Many companies came to the campus to host seminars and conduct interviews. The seminars with technology companies such as Google were too full; we had to draw lots. However, the career management person of the school had to convince students to go to seminars by Goldman Sachs or McKinsey. She said: "Please show some respect to them.

Please go and sit there, don't read the newspaper!" Even with that, the seminars on investment banking were half full.

I felt the great contrast of the mentality with my friends in the business schools on the East Coast. They called me and were keen to know the summer intern quota for Goldman Sachs and McKinsey. I told them that I honestly didn't know because nobody was interested. They told me that everybody on the East Coast was fighting to get into investment banks and consulting firms. I felt it was so far away. On the campus of Stanford, everybody was talking about start-ups and wanted to join a start-up. Suppose someone got a summer internship at Goldman Sachs or McKinsey. They would get the look of sympathy that they had no creativity and would work long hours in the offices. I was amazed at how much I had changed within less than a year.

Greater China Business Club

I knew my direction was to start my company in China by applying the knowledge and experience I learned in Japan and the US. However, I didn't have a clear idea of what to do. I thought that because I had left China for so long, the best way to understand the start-up scene in China was to be a venture capitalist.

Monitor Group offered me a job to research the VC and Private Equity market in China because they were evaluating the opportunity to take Monitor Clipper Partners Fund to China. I travelled to Beijing, Shanghai and Shenzhen and interviewed twenty venture capital and private equity firms. I compiled a report about the opportunities and key success factors of VC/PE investment in China. This was in 2003, right after SARS was settled down. There were no VC firms in Sandhill Road that entered China. I got permission to use the report. I hosted several seminars and visited many VC firms in Sandhill Road to convince them to go to China. There was no response.

In the second year, I realised many people had a common interest in China-related business opportunities. With four other students, we founded Greater China Business Club. Our mission was to be the bridge between the US and Greater China, which included not only mainland China but also Taiwan and Hong Kong. We hoped to build connections, accumulate knowledge and incubate businesses from the club. It immediately became one of the official student clubs because of the students' interest. We started having regular gatherings with business topic sharing. We invited guest speakers who were experienced in China-related businesses. Many people in Silicon Valley also joined our club because of the increased interest in China. We also invited successful entrepreneurs from China to speak at our events. Robin Li, the founder and CEO of Baidu, was one of the most famous speakers.

Make a difference!

Another year at Stanford quickly went by. Monitor Group liked what I did and gave me a full-time offer to join its China team to start its private equity investment in China.

Before graduation, a professor gave us a speech about opportunities in China. I asked: "What do you think is the opportunity in China that makes the most money?" the professor answered. "You are the smartest and brightest students in the world. It's easy for you to make money. However, I encourage you to try to make a difference rather than make money. Making a difference is a lot harder than making money. If you can make a difference, you should be able to figure out how to make money. However, even if you make a lot of money, you may not make a difference."

Make a difference. It was the motto of Stanford. I learned I should always try to use my talent to make a difference rather than make money.

LU DONG

Chapter 10
Joined a VC Firm in China

Reverse culture shock in China

In September 2004, I took Monitor Group's offer and returned to Beijing. It had been twelve years since I left. Everybody in my family was happy that I was back. I was excited to make a difference in China, leveraging what I had learned from Japan and the US.

However, after a couple of months, I started to feel frustrated. There were too many people in Beijing. The traffic was chaotic and noisy. Cars kept honking all the time and nobody obeyed the traffic rules. People spat on the street. On the train or bus, there was no private space. People kept pushing and touching me. Everyone was talking loudly in the restaurants. The service was slow and inadequate. The air was too polluted...

I was sick all the time. I felt I didn't want to go out. Instead, I stayed at home. I wasn't sure whether I made the right choice to go back to China. After living for twelve years in Japan and US, I wasn't used to living in China anymore. I had a reverse culture shock. I even thought about going back to Japan or US. I started missing the wide-open streets and fresh air in California, the quiet streets and the polite and swift service in Tokyo.

One day, I went to the street and again, someone spat in front of me. I looked sideways and frowned. However, when I looked around, I found nobody was bothered. People kept talking and laughing as if nothing happened.

I started to observe Chinese people around me. Despite the chaos, noise and pollution, people were happy. I was the only one who was not happy. I realised that the environment was not the problem. I was the problem. Nobody was bothered by the environment. Only I was bothered by the environment. However, at the same time, I realised I had a great opportunity because I could see the problems they couldn't see. From that moment, I became happy. I learned from Stanford that opportunities always come from solving pain points. Every pain I had became a potential opportunity.

GGV and HiSoft

Since Monitor Clip Partners didn't come as planned. I continued to work with Monitor Group as a consultant for a year. One day in 2005, I got a call from GGV Capital, a Sandhill Road VC firm. They remembered I visited them and tried to convince them to go to China. "Now we are ready to go to China. Do you want to be our first person in China?" the founding partner asked me. "Of course!" I said with great joy. Finally!

My first mission was to help manage one of GGV's portfolio companies, HiSoft, in Dalian. GGV made some great investments in later-stage technology companies in China, such as Baidu and Alibaba. However, HiSoft was its first investment in a series A company. HiSoft was a software outsourcing company with most of its clients in Japan. My job was sales, project management, M&A and raising series B for HiSoft. I had never worked in a start-up. I thought it was an excellent opportunity to get some operational experience. I moved to Dalian and worked day and night with the HiSoft team.

The founder Mr. Li grew up in Dalian. He studied Japanese and developed a software outsourcing business successfully. He was very humble and couldn't speak much English. GGV's style was hands-on. After making the investment, GGV helped the company hire a new management team after making the investment. The COO, HC, was a Malaysian hired from BCG. The CFO, Shuming, was an American Chinese hired from Credit Swiss. The CTO, Steve, was a Singaporean hired from HP. I got along with the new management team because their backgrounds were more like mine. I felt we all spoke the same language, not only English, but a similar business language. I also got along with the "old" founding team because I was Chinese. However, I felt the old and new management teams didn't speak the same language. Sometimes, I even felt the old founding team members felt inferior because they didn't get MBAs or speak English.

The VCs and the hired management had more seats on the board. Although I couldn't get into the board meetings, I felt there was tension at the meetings.

The new management created a super high-growth strategy to go IPO in two years on Nasdaq. The growth was not only through aggressive sales but also through mergers and acquisitions. We built an internal M&A team with a couple of associates from investment banks. In one year, we acquired three companies, one in Beijing, one in Shanghai and one in Hong Kong. After the acquisitions, two CEOs of the acquired companies joined the board. I felt the founder, Mr. Li became more and more frustrated.

After one year, the company more than tripled the number of employees. However, the revenues of all the group companies went down. We were in crisis.

One day, after some shouting in the conference room, Mr. Li raced out of the board meeting. Later that day, the CFO and CTO resigned, along with many team members. One week later, the board fired the CEO. Mr. Li and many of his loyal old founding team members also left. I had dinner with him and the other Chinese founders. He was sad and told me: "I wish you were one of us."

The board decided to lay off more employees in its Japan branch to cut costs. I flew to Japan with a board member; she was a Singaporean lady in her thirties. We held a board meeting in Japan. All other board members in Japan, excluding us, were Japanese men with grey hair. When the lady announced the layoff, the Japanese CEO in his seventies stood up and pondered the table. He was furious. I was the one translating between English and Japanese. "You are fired!" I said in Japanese.

MONEY, MONEY, MONEY

I went back to GGV and attended its annual off-site in Shanghai. I had the opportunity to meet with Thomas Ng, the founder of GGV Capital. Thomas was a Singaporean who spent more than twenty years in the US. He told me that in the US, VC was an apprenticeship business. You learned how to invest in start-ups by following experienced venture capitalists. "It's all about the people," he said. "When I met with founders of start-ups, I paid more attention to them outside the meeting rooms and observed their behaviours and saw how they treated other people. I ask myself; do I like him? Do I trust him? Do I respect him? No matter how attractive the business was, if I couldn't answer yes to the three questions about the founder, I wouldn't invest in the company," he continued. "For example, once, I met an entrepreneur who gave us a perfect presentation at our office. After the meeting, he drove us to visit his company. At a crossing, he ran a red light without hesitation. That was a deal breaker. If he ignored traffic rules, he could ignore other rules in business. I couldn't invest in such a person." He gave me more examples. "Another time, I heard an entrepreneur was cheating on his wife. I didn't invest in the company because if a man could cheat his wife, he could cheat anyone."

I asked him: "I have been back in China for two years and every CEO I met ignored traffic rules. They all went to KTV and played with girls. Some married men even brought their girlfriends to restaurants to have dinner with their friends. However, they all got investments from American VCs. I didn't like them. I didn't trust them. I didn't respect them. If we follow your rules, how can we invest in China?" "This is China," he answered. "We need to be flexible." "Then what rules can be compromised and what can't?" I asked him. "That's exactly what you need to learn," he smiled and replied.

Thomas gave a speech to all the partners, principals and associates at the offsite meeting. "We are venture capitalists. Do you know what the three things that venture capitalists do?" he asked. "Deal sourcing, due diligence and negotiation," I answered. "Wrong," he said and started writing on the flip board. "Number one, make money." He paused and looked around the room. "Number two, make money," he continued. "Number three, make money!" He wrote three big words. MONEY, MONEY, MONEY on the flip board. "The only thing venture capitalists do is make money. Never make mistakes by thinking you are friends of the entrepreneurs." I was shocked. "Isn't this the opposite of what the Stanford professor said?" I told myself. I lost motivation after hearing his speech. Also, I lost trust in him because he had a double standard when investing in companies between US and China.

To donate and be saved

Carrying a business card as a VC in China helped me meet many people. Wherever I went, people wanted to have meetings with me. I knew they were interested in the money rather than myself. However, the feeling of being important was still good.

I had an opportunity to attend an offsite with the EMBA students at Chong Kong Business School in Hainan. The EMBA programme of Chong Kong business school was famous because its students were among the most famous and wealthy CEOs in China.

After many luxurious banquets and KTV parties, one morning, we headed to a village to make donations to an elementary school. It was a small village by the Mountain Five Fingers. About ten CEOs, their assistants, reporters and cameramen got there by bus. I was shocked to see that the village was so poor. The elementary school was just a small house with a blackboard on the wall. There were no doors to the house. There were no desks or chairs. All the children were sitting on stones. The children barely had clothes to cover them. They were skinny and dark. The teachers looked more like farmers. Their clothes were old, dirty and broken. They reminded me of the people I saw in the documentary of Dr Muhammed Yunus.

When the CEOs got off the bus, their assistants put a big banner on the school's wall. After the CEOs made speeches, they handed the teachers donations, books, notepads, pencils and other stationery. They posed while shaking hands with the teachers while the cameramen were recording and taking pictures. I was shocked that the teachers and the students didn't react much. They didn't pose or smile in front of the cameras. Their facial expression was numb. I felt strange, but I didn't know why.

After the donation ceremony, it was about noon. The CEOs suggested we climb the famous Five Finger Mountain next to the school. As we climbed higher and higher, there was no trail anymore. It was a typical tropical forest in the mountain, hot and humid. We had to cut tree branches in our way. The roots of the trees were exposed above the ground, making it hard to walk. As the slope got steeper, we had to use our hands to grab the branches and roots to climb. Finally, after three hours of climbing, we reached the top of the mountain. We saw beautiful white clouds beneath us like the ocean. We took turns taking pictures and holding the EMBA banners. Everyone ate some food and drank some water we brought and took some rest.

We started heading downhill around 3:30pm. After about an hour, we realised we were much slower than climbing uphill. It was much harder going downhill on a tropical mountain. There were no trails and the mud and tree roots were slippery. The muscles of our legs were pumped up. At around 6pm, it started to become dark. We realised we still had a long way to go.

We were not prepared to climb a mountain like that, let alone at night. I didn't know we were going to climb the mountain beforehand. I was wearing a pair of Parada sneakers for street fashion. None of us brought a flashlight. We ate all our food and drank all the water at the top of the mountain. The worst was that there were no cellphone signals in the jungle. We couldn't even call for help.

We used the LED lights of our cell phones to light up the paths beneath our feet. One of the female assistants started cramping and couldn't walk. I massaged her legs and took turns with another guy helping her limp. She became despaired and started crying. We decided to rest and turn off the LED lights of our cell phones to save batteries.

Utter dark surrounded us. I couldn't even see my hands in front of my face. Suddenly, an unknown fear attacked my whole body. A chill runs down my back. I imagined a beast was staring at me in the darkness. Someone asked: "Are there snakes or leopards in the mountain?" A couple more females started to cry. "Calm down!" one of the CEOs shouted. "Even if there are any, there is nothing we can do. Let's go down!"

We lit up with our cell phones and started going down again. Soon, one after another, our cell phones ran out of batteries. At the same time, more and more people started to cramp. It was already around 9pm. We were hungry and thirsty. We were sweating in the humid tropical mountain. People kept moving slowly in the darkness, in silence with despair.

I felt we were powerless and helpless. They were the most powerful and wealthy CEOs in China. However, in nature, their thousands of employees and billions of dollars were so far away. Nothing, nobody could help us.

At around 11pm, we sent two guys who could move faster to go down the mountain and get help. We gave them one of two working cell phone lights. We saw them going down and the light disappeared in the darkness. I stayed with the group and we continued to move slowly downhill.

About one hour later, we saw some light moving quickly from below. It was the two teachers from the elementary school! They were running fast like black leopards in the jungles. One of them held a case of water. Another brought us some flashlights. One teacher dropped a case of water, put one of the limping ladies on his back and ran downhill. The other teacher handed us a couple of flashlights, put one limping lady on his back and ran downhill. They were small but fast. They gradually disappeared in the darkness. We drank some water, took some rest and used the flashlight to move downhill. It was much easier once we had some water and light.

Finally, at 1am, we all reached the bottom of the mountain. The teachers had already prepared some soup for us. We sat on the stones and drank the hot soup from a giant cauldron. The fire was made from wood. I am sure during the daylight, none of the CEOs would look at them and frown, but at that moment, we all felt it was one of the best meals in their lives.

I had a revelation at that moment. The CEOs, including myself, went to donate to the school, not because we cared about them but because we only wanted to feel good about ourselves. Deeply in our hearts, we were looking down on them. We donated because that gave us a sense of superiority. The people in the village had probably seen too much of this kind of hypocrisy. That's why they were not excited. However, they did all they could to rescue us when we were in trouble. Again, they didn't say much.

That night, I felt we were not there to save them; they saved us. The villagers may be poor in money but rich in hearts. We, the successful businesspeople in the big cities, were rich in money but poor in heart.

Why roads became narrower when you have more capabilities?

I had some friends who had a similar background to me in China. They studied and worked overseas. Now they are back in China to chase opportunities. We were called 海龟 in Chinese. It sounded like a sea turtle, but it meant someone returned from overseas. Many returnees worked in VC and PE industries.

One day there was a gathering of Chinese returnees who worked in the VC and PE industry. At my table, I heard them talking about their career paths. One person said: "It takes about four years in a VC firm to become a principal. Once you become a principal, you have two choices to become a partner. Either you move within your firm, or you join another firm. However, there are only a handful of VC firms in China. The partner position is limited. However, if you move to other industries, you can't make the same money. Investment banking and consulting work too long hours..."

Most of the young associates at the table seemed to agree with this theory. I felt the energy was very negative. It seemed the road ahead of them became narrower and narrower. Since there was no solution to this topic, then the topics became comparing the hotels and airlines they took when travelling business. They talked about the luxuries of certain hotel rooms and services in business classes among airlines.

I found myself utterly detached from the conversation. I was shocked because they were the most brilliant and educated people in China and those were the things they cared about. It was all about making money and spending money. Nobody talked about making a difference. The higher their education, income and seniority on the corporate ladder, the fewer their choices. I felt strange that it should be the opposite. I remembered the children in Hainan. Compared to them, the returnees should have more choices. Why their roads became narrower and narrower?

I realised their education, working experience and income had become their burdens instead of wings to help them fly higher.

Back at home, I reflected on how entrepreneurs struggled with VCs at HiSoft; the partner of GGV said, MONEY, MONEY, MONEY and fired the founders; the poor children and their teachers saved the CEOs from the mountain; the anguish of young professionals in VC and PE in China.

With the mindset of making more money by climbing the corporate ladder, fewer positions are available at the top. The choices became fewer and fewer.

However, with the mindset of making a difference, all the education, skills and experience I gained in the past only enable me to do more things in this world and be better.

I decided to let my education, skills and experiences become the wings to help me fly higher. I decided to be free from the rat-racing game by chasing positions in VC firms.

I decided to leave the money game and start my own company to create value for people in China by leveraging all I have learned in Japan, Goldman Sachs and Stanford.

Chapter 11
Start my First Company in China, Beyond Tailors: Shirts of Dell

Good to Great

I used what I learned at Stanford for ideas for my start-up. Passion first, strength second, then think about business models and most importantly, how my business benefits the people in China.

I started soul searching: what are my passions? I also didn't want my passion to go away soon. What can I do for ten years and still be passionate about it? I started searching for things I loved when I was a child.

I had been ordering tailored shirts, suits and coats in Beijing since returning to China. The fabrics were excellent and cheap. The tailors in Beijing were good and cheap, too. Once I found out I could have a shirt made for less than fifty dollars, a suit or a coat for two hundred dollars, I became interested in finding my favourite fabric in the fabric market in the suburb of Beijing. I often spent a whole day wandering among the hundreds of fabric merchants in the market and searching for my favourite fabric. I had a notepad with the business cards and samples of my favourite merchants glued to it. I also enjoyed reading fashion magazines and searching for my favourite designs.

After trying many tailors, I stayed with Mr. Zhou not only because of his craftsmanship, but also, he also came to my home to measure, listen to my design and deliver the products. It was very convenient.

Mr. Zhou came from a rural area in China. He had a small workshop in a two-bedroom apartment in a residential building in a suburb of Beijing. I had been to his place. There was much material piled in the room. There were a couple of sewing machines there. He and his wife worked hard day and night to maintain their living in Beijing while raising a daughter. He reminded me of my experience washing dishes in Japan. He was always diligent and humble. His price was reasonable among other tailors.

Most importantly, he was patient and truthful with my design instructions. I had a high standard for quality and specific requirements for design. For example, I used different colours of threads for the buttonholes; I had a specific requirement for the stiffness of the linings for collars. I had developed a unique pattern for shirts that when I raised my arms, the shirt wouldn't get pulled from my pants. Sometimes, when I was unsatisfied, I had him rework many times until I was satisfied.

Over the years, I introduced him to many of my friends. They all loved his products and services. I also supplied my friends with my designs and patterns. Mr. Zhou and I became friends.

One day in 2006, as usual, Mr. Zhou came to my apartment to deliver some finished products and to take some new orders. We had a good time chatting about fabric and design. I realised it was late for his last bus. Since his home was far from mine, he needed to take a bus for over one hour to get home. He said: "Don't worry, my driver is waiting in my car downstairs." "What?! You have a car and a driver?" "Yes," he said, thanks to my introductions, his business was flourishing. He just bought a car and hired a driver to visit his customers all over Beijing. I was shocked and curious at the same time. I always thought he was poor. "Can you walk me through how much money you are making?"

"Sure," he said. "I have about four hundred customers in Beijing. Each order five to ten shirts, two or three suits a year. I make one hundred yuan per shirt and eight hundred yuan per suit." "Wait," I opened the calculator app on my phone and did the maths. "So, you are making one million one hundred thousand yuan a year?" I almost shouted, realising he was making more money than I did as an associate in a VC firm. "Something like that. I also hired five workers to ramp up the production so I can focus on customer relationships."

The business plan

I realised I had the business I was looking for at that moment! I realised I had always been passionate about fashion since high school. In terms of strength, I was better than Mr. Zhou in design and marketing. Furthermore, I could use the internet to expand the business faster and more broadly. Finally, the money. Mr. Zhou had already proved that. If he could gain four hundred customers in Beijing in two years, I could gain one hundred times or ten thousand times more than him by leveraging my marketing and internet skills.

That night, I drafted the business plan for my first business. I gave it a name, Beyond Tailors. My idea was to mass-customise shirts at a reasonable price for professionals online and we deliver them to your home. It's the "Shirts of Dell".

I thought everyone had different body sizes and preferences. However, the mass-manufactured shirts are priced reasonably, but they are not personalised. On the other hand, tailored shirts fit personal needs but were expensive. I could create a website where people could personalise their shirts by choosing designs and fabrics and inputting sizes. I could have Mr. Zhou make them and ship them to the world.

"Beyond Tailor shirts are more personalised than off-the-rack shirts, cheaper than branded shirts and more convenient than traditionally tailored shirts." I even created the slogan.

I quickly created a business plan and financial projection. I had a meeting with Mr. Zhou and told him my plan. I told him: "Get ready to hire more workers. I am going to place a lot of orders for you." Mr. Zhou was excited and agreed to be my manufacturing base.

I needed to build a website and design product offerings and packaging. I needed some funding for purchasing fabrics as inventory. However, I wasn't ready to raise funding from VCs because I thought I wanted to do it more conservatively since it was my first start-up. I wanted to bootstrap by using my savings for the central part. I had about five hundred thousand yuan in savings. However, I still needed some outside funding. The first investors were three Fs: Family, friends and fools. I talked to one of my Stanford classmates and best friend, Shauna. Shauna and her husband, Sean, liked the idea.

They decided to invest one hundred thousand yuan and offer a room in the office of their family business.

The recruiting

Next, I needed a team: a graphic designer, a programmer and an assistant for the operation. I started searching for talents in the entrepreneur circle in Beijing. At the same time, I was giving speeches and lectures at the top universities in Beijing about my experience in investment banking, consulting and MBA because those were the dreams of many students in China.

One day, I gave a speech at the University of International Business and Economics to about one hundred students. At the end of the speech, I advertised my new start-up idea. I told the students I was hiring. I welcomed students to work for me, even on a part-time basis. I wrote my email on the blackboard. There were about ten students showed interest. I gave them my business cards. In the next two days, I got about five emails. Two students wanted to have an interview for the job.

It was about 4pm when Nana Zhao walked into my office. She told me about her stories. She grew up in Northern China. Her mum died when she was small. She came to Beijing by getting into UIBE, one of the top universities to study finance. After one hour, I told her I liked her background. It resonated with my experience of going to Japan alone and struggling to live and study by supporting myself. "However," I said. "You and I are too similar. We are both in finance. I would rather have a person who knows the areas of apparel and supply chain management which I don't know." She agreed and left with disappointment.

When I woke up the following day, there was an email with an 11-page research report in my mailbox. It was from Nana. She wrote: "I spent a night researching the shirt market and manufacturing. I still don't know a lot about the fashion business online. However, I can learn. If you give me an opportunity, I can prove that I can be an expert in those areas." Her attitude deeply touched me. Now, I had my first employee. Since she was already in the second year of her master's degree, she had plenty of time outside classes. She started working for me four days a week.

Another undergraduate student from UIBE, Yongfeng Feng also interviewed and joined the company part-time.

From the introductions of entrepreneurs, I also hired a manager and a graphic designer who used to work at an internet start-up. Now I had a five-person team.

Apprentice in Hong Kong

While the team was working on the website, I went to Hong Kong to study tailoring and source fabrics. A famous tailor in Hong Kong had been in business for over fifty years. His sales agents were around the world. The agents were trained with his measurement method to work anywhere in the world, take their clients' measurements and send the measurements to the tailor shop in Hong Kong. The tailor had a big workshop with many workers to manufacture shirts, suits and coats.

The workshop could put the agent's labels on the products and ship them to the agents. The agents then delivered the products to their clients and do the fittings. I could use this method to do my online tailoring business. Not only had I learned how to take measurements of clients, but also the manufacturing process. Hong Kong was known as a trading centre for the best fabrics in the world. I secured several shops supplying European fabrics by the cut length. I took their sample fabric books and put down a deposit with them. Every time I ordered, I just needed to email them the number of fabrics and the length. They would cut that fabric's length and mail them to Beijing. The shipping fee was only about twenty Hong Kong dollars per package.

Back in Beijing, I also found suppliers for buttons and lining. I also designed the label and packaging, had them made and shipped to me.

Within a couple of months, we launched the business. Customers could choose designs for collars, cut patterns and sleeves on the website. Then, customers chose the fabrics. We offered three grades of fabrics: Chinese fabrics for three hundred and ninety yuan, Italian fabrics for five hundred and ninety yuan and branded British fabrics for seven hundred and ninety yuan. Our prices were about one-third of the price to buy the same grade shirts in a department store. Finally, customers needed to input their measurements for neck, shoulder width, chest, waist, height and weight. We asked for their body types as well. We offered embroideries of customers' names in different colours and fonts in different places on the shirt. We offered global shipping so that we could reach customers worldwide.

I sent invitations to many of my Stanford classmates and friends in banking, consulting, auditing and law firms with a discount to try out our products. Orders started to come in. We sent the purchase orders of fabrics to suppliers in Hong Kong and China and had them delivered to Mr. Zhou. At the same time, we sent Mr. Zhou the order number and measurement data. The turnaround time was about two days. We got the final products from Mr. Zhou. We packaged them and shipped them to our customers.

Our cash flow was positive because our customers paid us first and we had no inventory. The profit margins for our shirts ranged from fifty per cent to sixty-five per cent. However, initially, we gave discounts to new customers, which lowered our margin.

Changing business models

After a couple of months, we got feedback that people found it hard to measure themselves. Also, they would like to touch the fabrics in person before purchase. I realised the limitations of online tailoring. We were the first company that did online shirt tailoring in Asia. There was another company Vancl, that sold off-the-rack shirts online. We were the pioneers in selling male shirts online in China in 2006.

I decided to change our office location to the Central Business District area in Beijing and use our office as a showroom and a shop. We made sample shirts in different designs and sizes for people to try. We had sample fabrics for people to touch and feel. Most importantly, we took measurements for the customers.

When people walked around the office buildings in the morning or lunch hour, we passed flyers to them to advertise our services. Soon, the business grew steadily. I learned from Mr. Zhou to offer visiting services to reach more potential customers. We went to our customers' places to take measurements and deliver products. We hired about ten sales agents around Beijing to visit our customers.

The bottleneck

However, as we got more and more orders, the quality became worse and worse. Initially, the defective rate was ten per cent when we got ten orders daily. We had to return the defective shirt to Mr. Zhou to fix the problems. However, it became worse and worse. I had many meetings with Mr. Zhou to think about ways to keep the quality under control. However, one day, we got one hundred orders per day. The defective rate became one hundred per cent. There was a shirt delivered to us without any buttonholes.

It was a crisis for us. I called Mr. Zhou to discuss the situation. He looked at the defective shirts and cried. He said: "Sorry for the trouble. However, this is really beyond my capability. I had to hire more and more workers to keep up with your increasing orders. However, it took time to train them. Also, I couldn't monitor every worker all the time. I just don't know how to do it..." I realised this was something Mr. Zhou had never done. It was beyond his capabilities. He was a tailor but didn't have experience in mass manufacturing.

I searched and found many tailors around Beijing to have them make shirts for me. However, I still couldn't completely get rid of the defection. How did Dell do mass customisation? I started studying Dell's model and manufacturing in the apparel industry. I found out that although every Dell computer may be different, the assembly lines were relatively simple, putting the standard parts together. However, every shirt required human hands to sew pieces of materials together. The human involvement was much more than assembling computers. After all, no machines could automatically make a shirt without human involvement, even today.

In mass apparel manufacturing, orders were in the hundreds and thousands. The line workers only work on a few processes of the entire manufacturing process. As the line workers made repetitive movements, they became better and better at doing them. The defective rate became lower and lower. That was how the factories could produce high-quality products. However, in the tailoring manufacturing process, not only is every order different but also one worker typically completes the whole manufacturing process for one shirt. The requirements for the workers were more complex, which made the tailored products more expensive. Also, since the tailoring workers didn't get to practice repetitively, quality control became very difficult when the volume increased. I realised I faced a problem that the entire apparel industry couldn't solve for the past hundred years.

Making a difference with the shirt

One year into my tailoring business, a man walked into my showroom with his friend. He wore a beautiful pink shirt. He was knowledgeable about our products and explained how to choose the fabric to his friend. I was fascinated and praised the man. "Thank you for helping us. Your shirt is beautiful. It fitted you perfectly and the pink colour made you look healthy." He smiled at me and spoke: "Do you remember that one year ago you made me this shirt? At that time, I knew nothing about fashion. The shirt you made for me got me a lot of praise from my colleagues. I gained a lot of confidence and became interested in fashion." He continued: "Now I am trying to help my colleague make a shirt too!" I remembered him. He looked like a different person when he first walked into our shop last year. Now, he was utterly changed. He looked handsome and confident. I tried to hold the tears in my eyes. It was the first time I felt my work made a difference in someone's life.

The realisation

Another realisation was that although the concept of mass customisation was good, tailored shirts were a niche market. I found out only two kinds of people had a demand for tailored shirts. One was people who had difficulty finding off-the-rack shirts because their body shapes differed dramatically from ordinary people. The other type was the fashion-conscious, so they had specific requirements for shirts that were hard to find with off-the-rack shirts. Both of those people were a small percentage of the market. Most people were satisfied with the designs and sizes of off-the-rack shirts. Ordinary people didn't have much demand for tailored shirts.

Understanding the challenges of tailoring business from both supply and demand sides, I had two choices to make. One was to keep doing tailored shirts and try to solve the supply chain problem. The other was to apply what I learned to other product categories. I decided to pursue option two because I didn't think I could solve the supply chain problem in a short time and I wanted to build a business that serves the main market instead of a niche market.

I found other interesting data from our orders. Although we only offered products for males, twenty per cent of our customers were females. Often, a lady would drag her special others to our showroom to get measured.

I thought since female apparel is a much bigger market, I should look for product categories in the female apparel industry. Also, I was looking for new retail business models other than store-based models in US and Japan.

After some research, I found two companies that rose on top of my list, Victoria's Secret in the US and Cecile in Japan. Both companies sold female underwear through mail orders. They created record sales exceeding any store-based brands in each country. The reason was that female underwear had a high repeat rate and high margin. Once customers found the fit of certain underwear, they tend to keep purchasing the same products for a long time. Mail order model was more convenient for consumers because didn't need to go to the stores.

The mail-order model was in the past. The online direct marketing model was superior to mail orders. At that time, there were no female underwear brands doing online direct marketing in China. Bingo! I found a new opportunity!

LU DONG

Chapter 12
Start my Second Company in China: La Miu, the Victoria's Secret of China

The angel investors

At the beginning of 2008, I quickly drafted a business plan. The title was "The Victoria's Secret of China". I was confident that the business could be much more significant. I was targeting the primary market, female underwear. There were successful examples in the US and Japan. There was no one doing it in China. And China's consumers were ready for it because the eCommerce business started a few years ago. Most importantly, I already had two years of experience in online apparel retail through Beyond Tailors.

I know I was ready to raise much bigger funds from professional investors this time. I contacted two tycoons in Japan who were clients at Goldman Sachs. Mikitani-san was the founder and CEO of Rakuten, the largest eCommerce platform in Japan. Shigeta-san was the founder and CEO of Japan's largest mobile phone distribution network. Each of them had a net worth of more than two billion dollars. Both had made some investments in China's technology companies.

Mikitani-san agreed to meet me in Tokyo. Sitting in his office, I handed him my business plan. I started telling my stories, from founding Beyond Tailors to why I wanted to change my business model to female underwear online retail. He quickly flipped through the pages. I was unsure whether I should speak faster to keep up with his pace. I started to get nervous. "So, how much money do you need?" Mikitani-san asked after flipping through the deck. "One million dollars," I answered. "OK! If you don't give up, you will succeed!" He smiled at me and nodded to his investment manager. Within thirty minutes, I got one million dollars of investment from the founder of Japan's most successful eCommerce company! I was so excited.

I went to visit Shigeta-san. It was even easier this time. Shigeta-san knew that Mikitani-san had invested one million dollars. He also decided to put in one million dollars.

The secret of Victoria's Secret

Returning to China, I decided to close Beyond Tailors and focus on this new company doing female underwear. There were few synergies between the two companies. I talked to a few investors in Beyond Tailors about my decision and promised to allocate them shares from my personal shares in the new company. I also talked to the employees about my decision. By then, Nana and Yongfeng had graduated from UIBE and joined me full-time. They were excited about the new opportunity. I kept one salesperson to keep servicing the existing customers of Beyond Tailors.

I needed a brand name for this female underwear brand. I had been thinking about it day and night. I considered my aspiration to return to China to make a difference. I remembered when I researched the female underwear market, all the brands and products looked similar in every department store I went to. Nothing was exciting and inspiring. However, Victoria's Secret stores were big. The designs of the store and the packaging were stylish. Most importantly, the lingerie shows every year was like a big celebration.

The key word was sexy. I realised Victoria's Secret wasn't selling underwear. They were selling dreams for women to be sexy. The shows were not about the lingerie; it was a celebration of sexiness. "What is the definition of sexy?" I asked myself. I felt it was both physical and mental. The angles of Victoria's Secret were the image ambassadors of sexiness. Not only were they sexually appealing physically, but also their energy was positive, vibrant and confident. That was the definition of sexiness in the American way. That was the secret of Victoria's Secret.

I felt I understood the key success factor of Victoria's Secret. It was the success of a combination of branding and business model. I didn't want to simply copy Victoria's Secret to China. The sexy appeal of Victoria's Secret was too explicit in China, which I found out after research. The mail-order model might not fit China. I wanted to learn the essence of success and create a brand and business model that fitted the market in China.

La Miu: Sexiness is my attitude.

One night, I woke up at 3am in dreams and a name popped into my mind. La Miu. I looked up the domain name. lamiu.com was available. I immediately registered it.

I had been thinking about what kind of difference I wanted to make in the female underwear market in China. I realised although there were more than three thousand underwear factories in China. China made eighty per cent of the bras in the world. However, there was no brand. What is a brand? A brand is a name that gives people emotional benefits. A product gives people functional benefits. Dr. Kotler said: "Good companies sell products; excellent companies sell brands."

I determined to create a brand that gave Chinese females dreams so that they could be the best of themselves. That's why I thought of the name La Miu.

Miu meant muse. In Greek mythology, a muse is one of nine goddesses who preside over the arts and sciences, inspiring creativity and guiding artists and thinkers. Each muse is associated with a particular area of expertise, such as music, poetry, or history. I thought every woman was born into this world with unique talents. No matter the talents, each talent was beautiful in its own way.

I thought many women might not live up to the best of themselves because they didn't realise their unique talents and beauty. Those talents might be hidden inside her. Underwear was just like their talents, hidden under clothes. Not known by others. Only she knew her talents.

I wanted to create a brand and use underwear to awaken women's sleeping talents and beauty so that they could be the best of themselves, uniquely beautiful.

I also created a brand slogan after deciding on the brand name and concept. "Sexiness is my attitude." The advertising design was like the design of the iPod posters. The background was a solid colour. There was a black and white portrait of a person, a woman, or a man, wearing bras on her body or covering part of his face. At the bottom, the slogan "性感就是我的态度" was written. The branding was so controversial that instantly, it became a hit on the market.

Designed in Tokyo, made in China.

I knew having co-founders who had skills that were complementary to mine was the key to success. I needed three experts to get the business started. An expert experienced in online marketing in China, an underwear expert who knew design and manufacture and a branding design expert from Japan to keep building the foundation of the branding experience. I found two co-founders out of the three areas I needed. Jianyao Hao had been working in a start-up in Beijing doing internet marketing after graduating from a college in Russia. His role in the company was product, marketing and operation. Daisuke Kanazu studied in Japan, China and US and was well-connected in the design circle in Japan. His role was branding, visual merchandising and manufacturing. Because Tokyo was the centre of fashion in Asia, we created the entire branding and visual merchandising design in Tokyo. All our models were from Japan. The photo shootings were also done in Tokyo. On the labels and packaging, it was written: Designed in Tokyo, made in China.

We found OEM factories across China made bras for Japanese brands such as Wacoal, Peach John and Aimerfeel. Some factories also manufactured for Victoria's Secret. We required them to manufacture bras for us with the same qualities as Japanese and US brands.

The Shocks

15 July, 2008, after six months of preparation, we went online. Everyone in the office was waiting for the first order. At 11am, we got our first order. We were betting on how many orders we could get on the first day. The orders kept getting in. Our ordering hotline kept ringing. We had a very busy day. Finally, we got a total of one hundred and sixty-two orders for the first day. It was a big success! We were jumping and shouting in the office.

We shocked the underwear industry in China. An industry person told me later. Neither the consumers nor the Chinese underwear manufacturers had seen anything like La Miu. La Miu was so unique in its branding, design and sales model. We were the first underwear brand in China that was born online.

Our orders kept growing day by day. However, after one month, twenty websites in China had started copying us. Two websites even cloned everything including our pictures and products. They just changed the logos. Two out of the twenty websites even got funding from VCs.

Another month passed. Lehman Shock broke out. Within six months, since there was no funding, most of our copycats disappeared. One of the two copycats went bankrupt. They came to us and asked us to buy their inventories at twenty per cent of their cost. We bargained to ten per cent and bought some of their inventories.

Luckily, seeing the initial success, the angel investors added two million dollars more funding to us. We were one of the few companies in China that had cash on hand during the Lehman Shock. When most companies withdrew their online advertising, the advertising price dropped. We put two million dollars into online advertising. Our sales skyrocketed. Later, we found out we were the number two online advertiser in China in 2008.

We heard feedback from customers that they wanted to try and fit before purchasing our bras. I understood their needs with my experience from Beyond Tailors. We opened physical stores six months after launching our online store.

Breaking the rules and record

We had Japanese designers design our first store in China. It was in 西单君太百货 Grand Pacific Department store. We designed our store to be four times larger than other underwear brands on the same floor. We spent four times the construction cost per square metre compared to the industry standard. We were the first underwear brand to put a forty-five-inch LED TV in the store to play our photo-shooting videos. Some industry people told me we would never make money because we broke all the rules in the underwear industry. They said we didn't have any experience and didn't know the rules in the underwear industry.

We hired six sales ladies who had underwear sales experience before. We invited a trainer from Japan to train them with a service level equal to Japan. The training course was one week. On the third day, the trainer asked me if she could fire one of the sales ladies. Her negative attitude influenced other team members. I agreed. At the final presentation of the sales training, each sales lady demonstrated the service. They were professional and confident. I was shocked to see how much people could change within a week! My dream was to provide Japanese quality service to consumers in China. It came true! I stood up and applauded. The sales ladies and the trainer were shouting, jumping and hugging each other. They cried like they had won Olympic gold medals.

We had the best store and the best sales ladies on the underwear floor among twenty other brands. We also drove traffic from online to our store with sales campaigns. After six months, not only did our store break even and start to generate profit, but also, we were the number one sales among twenty underwear brands.

Burn money and grow!

In three years, we opened twelve stores in Beijing, Shanghai, Qingdao and Hong Kong. In every location, we repeated our success.

Online sales grew six hundred per cent year on year for the first three years. In addition to our own web store, we sold our products on major eCommerce platforms in China such as Taobao.com and Jingdong.com.

We increased the suppliers to forty factories across China to catch up with the sales. We opened a manufacturing office in Guangdong to coordinate with the factories.

To keep up with the growth, we expanded our warehouse three times. In 2011, our warehouse was twenty thousand square metres in a suburb in Beijing.

The number of employees grew from ten to three hundred in three years. There was always a line in front of our HR department for interviews.

The highlight was our lingerie shows. Victoria's Secret had lingerie shows once a year. We held lingerie shows and parties every month in various places in Beijing. Many famous clubs invited us to have lingerie shows at their places. Our biggest one was at an outdoor plaza in Sanlitun, the most happening place in Beijing for fashionable young people. It was a hot summer night. Not only did we have thousands of people watching the show on-site. We also invited many famous Social Network leaders to broadcast the show live from their personal accounts to fifty million users online.

La Miu was a phenomenon in China. I was on many magazines and TV shows and was invited to speak at many events. I felt my dream came true.

Behind all the growth was a massive capital injection from venture capital firms. We raised twenty million dollars from Silicon Valley VC firms and Japanese VC firms. We joined the race of growth and dreamed IPO in five years. The VC partners joined our board. They were pushing us to grow faster. "You only grew six hundred per cent year on year. Look at Vancl, the shirt online retailer, they grew two thousand per cent. Just burn as much money as possible and grow faster!" The market after the Lehman Shock recovered quickly. eCommerce was booming. There were hundreds of eCommerce companies that got VC funding. The mood of the entire market was to grow the top line. Nobody was interested in creating profit.

Every Monday morning, we had a town hall meeting. Learned from Amazon, we always started with the customer service centre. One day, one person from customer service read an email from a customer. She projected the email with a picture attachment to the big screen. The letter was from a newly married young woman. She said she had been a shy girl in college. She wasn't confident about herself at all. One day, she encountered La Miu. The bra and the brand concept gave her confidence. She started to pay attention to herself and became more attractive. She met her boyfriend soon after. Now she has just got married happily to her boyfriend. She attached her wedding picture to her email. She thanked La Miu for changing her life. She was wearing La Miu's bras under the wedding dress. She would never forget about La Miu and continue to hope La Miu can give her hope and happiness in her life.

Tears came out of my eyes. I looked around; there were many people in the office weeping. We were swamped every day. However, I felt we made a difference in her life at that moment. That was worth all the hard work we put in.

The downfall

In 2012, the eCommerce bubble burst in China. No VCs would invest in eCommerce companies that didn't have profit. That meant ninety-nine per cent of the eCommerce companies couldn't get funding. Hundreds of eCommerce companies went bankrupt. A few big ones with cash reserves started to downsize and acquire their competitors.

We calculated that we only had six months of cash runway. The management went through the P/L repeatedly to see where we could cut costs and preserve cash. The only four areas were advertising, salary, rent and factory account payables. We decided to cut advertising fees to zero, cut salary to one-third, move our office to reduce the rent by seventy per cent and delay account payables to pay only ten per cent to the key factories every month gradually.

We still had a huge pile of inventory in our warehouse. The most painful experience was to let go of two hundred out of three hundred people in the company. I got laid off by Goldman Sachs. Now, I was on the other side of the table. The two co-founders and most of the top management left. It was not pleasant at all. Some of them still hate me and don't talk to me to this day.

The delaying of account payables damaged our suppliers. Many factories couldn't pay their workers and went out of business. Delivery companies didn't have enough packages to deliver and fired many employees. One day, I visited one of our primary delivery companies to negotiate the pricing. The CEO had a big scar on his face. He told me that in the middle of a talk about laying off an employee, the employee suddenly stabbed him in the face and chest with a knife. The CEO got carried to the ER immediately and survived. He was lucky because the wound on his chest was only a centimetre from his heart. He just got out of the hospital recently.

At a board meeting, the VC partner pounded the table, pointed his finger at me and shouted: "You are the shame of Stanford!"

I felt every day was like a dark winter day. Every day was survival. I had to deal with angry and sad employees, suppliers, board members and shareholders. Every day was firefighting. I had no vision of the end of the tunnel. I couldn't eat or sleep. My gastritis came back.

On top of that, I could only sleep once every other day. This created a vicious circle. During the day, my productivity and EQ became worse, thus delaying problems and producing more problems. Too many things clogged my mind. My head became heavy. I felt like I was wearing a heavy helmet. All the noise was like a big traffic jam in my brain at night. I wished I had a switch to turn it off, but I couldn't. I was dragging myself to work every day like a zombie.

The worst day

Finally, one day, on my way home, I thought, what am I doing? I was trying to make a difference and do what I love. However, I didn't remember when I started chasing fame and money. My goals became fundraising and IPO. I brainwashed myself with my own talk to the media about how great we were. I tried to make customers happy, investors happy, suppliers happy and employees happy, but I ignored my wife and family. Most importantly, I didn't make myself happy. I was completely exhausted.

I went home and felt I was a complete failure and powerless. I hadn't been back home for dinner for three months. I sat with my wife and said: "Sorry to leave you alone at home for so long. I promised to give you a happy life. I can't. Now, the company is about to go bankrupt. It's over."

To my surprise, my wife didn't get sad. She held my hands and spoke: "Today may be the worst day in your life, but I can live like this for the rest of my life. You may lose everything, but you have me. We love each other. We are smart. We can start over and do anything." Tears gushed out of my eyes. I hugged her and cried for a long time.

At the next town hall meeting, I spoke to the remaining 100 people in a small office. I looked around. The mood was low and everybody was nervous. I told the team: "I am sorry for letting go of the other teammates. It's not their fault. It's not your fault. It's my fault. I take total responsibility as the CEO. We didn't create profit but relied on VC funding to fuel growth for the past three years. However, the weather has changed. We are in winter now. We need to survive together to get through the winter. We still have three million customers, we still have our brand, we have tons of inventories and we still have our online and offline stores. Most importantly, we have each other. We love each other, we are smart. We can figure out ways to not only survive but thrive."

The team stayed together to figure out the survival plan.

After cutting the advertising fees to zero, our sales dropped to half. We changed our mindset that we didn't rely on costly advertising, instead, we focused on our existing customers. We analysed existing customers about their preferences and pain points. We created a CRM program to send personalised emails to existing customers and recommend them products based on their purchasing. We encouraged them to refer their friends and get rewards. Thanks to our core customers' repeat purchases, we reached break-even. We grew slowly but steadily.

Realised the change in myself

I reflected that I changed from customer focus to investor focus when we raised funds from VC firms and had VC partners on our board. Unconsciously, I shifted from serving customers to serving shareholders. I wanted to make shareholders happy by pushing the company to grow fast and big and go IPO quickly. However, our customers didn't care how fast or big we are and neither did they care if we were a public company or not. Our customers only cared about the quality of our products and services. Our products and services were media to convey our love. If we love our customers by providing them with the best products and services, they would love us back by voting for us with their cash. It was so simple.

We had initial success because we poured our hearts into making a difference in our customers' lives. The result was growth in orders. However, when we made money, the VCs invested in us. I changed my focus to making our investors happy instead of continuing to make our customers happy. I was shocked to realise I was blind about my change.

I remembered Steve Jobs when he gave a speech to us at Stanford GSB. No wonder why he spent the whole time showing us how great the new iPod was. Fundamentally, Steve Jobs was a product manager. He focused on his customers and products. He had such a deep insight into customers' needs. Steve Jobs believed that successful products were often created by anticipating and meeting the needs of customers before they even realised those needs existed. It was like if Henry Ford had listened to the customers' feedback and created a product according to their request, he would have created a faster carriage instead of a car.

I analysed why I changed my focus from customers to investors.

First, it was easier for me. Because of my background in finance, it was much easier for me to talk to investors than to the manufacturers. There were only two ways to get the money in the bank for start-ups, make money or raise money. Making millions of dollars by selling one pair of bras at a time was hard. However, to me, raising money in millions of dollars was relatively easy. Human instincts make me do easy things automatically. If I don't intentionally do the hard but right things, I would just follow my human instincts and do the easy things.

Second, I created an environment to pay more attention to shareholders than customers. When the company grew larger, I had less contact with the customers. I had regular board meetings which represented shareholders' interests. The influence from shareholders was regular and powerful. Not to mention I had frequent meetings with bankers, auditors and lawyers to plan for IPO. Those people and meetings became my main environment. Humans are products of the environment. When I was surrounded by VCs and bankers, I think and talk more like a banker. I remembered a quote, the strategy of a company was not the PowerPoint slides that the CEO created, but where the CEO spent time.

After realising that, I implemented some changes in the company. We held regular customer focus groups. I was there every time. We had regular internal rotation among team members so that everyone had exposure to our customers. For example, all our team members must either spend one day at our stores or at our customer call centre to see or talk to our customers. Every Thursday, everyone in the company, regardless of male or female would wear a pair of bras to work. We really experienced how our customers feel about our products.

The most significant change was I resigned from the CEO position and promoted Xiaomei Li to be the CEO. She had been playing a vital role in the restructuring and turning around of the company. Before joining our company, she had twenty years of retail and manufacturing experience in the lingerie industry. She was brave to take on the role of VP of Operation right after we downsized. Over three years of hardship, she never complained and worked hard. She became a role model for all team members. Most importantly, she had the same vision and mission as me: to use our products and services to convey love to the females in China and to use our brand to make a difference in their lives.

I was ready to move on. I recalled Try Me, the international club I founded at Saitama University. I was the founder and the leader. However, I must give the leadership role to the next generation because I had to graduate from college. I felt the same with La Miu. The founder's role was to start the company from zero to one. My most important role was to build the company's vision, mission and value. As Jim Collins said in Good to Great, the most important thing was getting the right people onto the bus. After La Miu had been born with a groundbreaking brand concept and business model, growing rapidly with VCs' capital injection, downsizing and re-focusing on customers in the past six years, it now had a solid manufacturing base. Most importantly, the company had a mature team that learned valuable lessons through the journey. Nana became the Vice President of the company. She worked in almost all departments except programming. We didn't have high-paying executives who had MBA degrees or overseas experiences. However, everyone had a deep understanding of our customers in China. They loved what they did, which was not only making and selling underwear but also inspiring changes of hearts in China's females so that they could be the best of themselves.

In 2014, one of our underwear manufacturers approached us to acquire our company. They had manufacturing capabilities but didn't have a brand or sales channels. At the same time, La Miu struggled with manufacturing with our OEM factories because they were too fragmented and it was difficult to control quality. Seeing the synergies, the shareholders agreed on the sale of the company.

I felt I did what I aimed for. I built a brand and team in China. Together, we made a difference in China's retail and underwear industry. We made a difference among Chinese females.

Chapter 13
Start my Third Company in Japan: TakeMe, Copy From China

In July 2014, we exited China, both my business and my family. We moved back to Tokyo.

Identified the new opportunity

Soon, I surprisingly realised the smartphone services and apps which were very convenient in China were not available in Japan, such as food delivery apps, restaurant reservation apps, bicycle ride-sharing apps, taxi apps, mobile battery rental apps, QR-code payment apps and restaurant ordering apps. After smartphones came into being in 2007, China leapfrogged the West and gave birth to many innovative business models. Living in big cities in China, people only needed a smartphone for everything in their lives. I felt it was inconvenient living in Tokyo.

I had friends come to Japan every month. I found the common theme was that they all asked me for recommendations and reservations for restaurants. I found there was no website for foreigners to find and reserve restaurants in Japan. I created a PowerPoint with my personally recommended restaurants in popular areas in Tokyo. My friends appreciated my support and said they couldn't have had such a great experience without my help.

At the same time, I was sad to see many good Japanese restaurants go out of business because of the lack of capabilities to generate customers.

I had a eureka moment for a new business opportunity! The pain points for dining for foreign tourists in Japan were in four areas: they couldn't find good local restaurants, there were no mobile apps for foreign tourists to make reservations, they couldn't order in Japanese restaurants and finally, they couldn't pay using mobile payment apps. Eighty per cent of retail in Japan was paid by cash. Most of the restaurants only take cash. Credit cards were not popular, not to mention mobile payments. QR-code payment didn't exist in Japan.

In China, there were apps to solve those pain points. I could just copy the mobile services products and business models from China to Japan and solve the problems.

Restaurants wanted to have foreign tourists as customers because they spend more than the locals. However, the owners and staff of Japanese restaurants didn't know how to attract foreign tourists to their restaurants. Furthermore, most of the staff working in restaurants didn't speak foreign languages.

I felt the new business idea was perfect for me by applying the model in From Good to Great. First, in terms of purpose and passion, the business benefited the normal people in both China and Japan. Since both China and Japan were my home countries, I had always been passionate about creating businesses that benefit people in both countries. Also, I loved travelling and dining. How great it was to turn my passion into a business. Second, in terms of strength, I could leverage my experience in online and offline retail technology and apply it to the restaurant industry. Furthermore, cross-border business is difficult intrinsically because it requires a deep understanding of business, culture and language to do business in multiple countries. It created a natural competitive moat for other companies to copy. Third, in terms of money, the restaurant industry in Japan was twenty-four trillion yen (approximately two hundred and twenty billion US dollars). If we only got one per cent of the market share, it was already two billion dollars. The business model was proven in China by many restaurant tech companies. The revenue could come from the revenue sharing with restaurants or SaaS.

Started Japan Foodie

I quickly put together a business plan. I gave this new company a name, Japan Foodie. The slogan was: your best local friend. My goal was to create an app for foreign tourists to be their best local friends to help them find, reserve, order and pay at restaurants when they travel to Japan.

I raised one hundred million yen from friends in Japan and China. My co-founder and I worked hard for six months to convince one hundred restaurants to be on our platform.

In July 2016, we successfully launched the app Japan Foodie. It was the first app for foreign tourists to find, reserve and pay at restaurants in Japan.

The app had about three hundred restaurants in Tokyo. It had beautiful pictures of Japanese food, such as yakiniku and sushi. Users could look for restaurants based on locations on maps and sort by categories, pricing and rankings. Users could make reservations by choosing the date and time and inputting the number of people. We would confirm with the restaurant for availability. All reservations were prepaid to prevent no-shows. The app was in English, Simplified and Traditional Chinese and Japanese. The app also had a wallet function built in. Using the scanner of the app, users could scan a QR code at the restaurant and pay with credit cards, Apple Pay, or other QR code-based eWallets in China.

We kept growing the number of restaurants, downloads and reservations. I raised another one hundred-million-yen pre-A round from more investors. This time, a few public companies invested in us strategically.

Pivot from B2C to B2B

However, I found a problem with our business model. Because we were targeting foreign tourists in Japan, it was very hard for the lifetime value of a user to cover the acquisition cost.

The breakthrough was we decided to work with Chinese travel apps to enable reservations for Japan's restaurants on their apps and abandon our own app. This created a multiple-winning situation. Chinese tourists could use the travel apps to reserve restaurants in Japan with no need to download a new app, Japan Foodie. Chinese travel apps could provide more functions and make more money for their users. Restaurants in Japan got more reservations through huge traffic from Chinese travel apps. Finally, we didn't need to spend time and money to acquire users and had immediate traffic from Chinese travel apps.

The result was dramatic. The orders increased thirty times in one month. We only needed to focus on the operation of the order processing by working with the Chinese tourists and restaurants. Also, because of the solid track records, sales to restaurants became much easier.

TakeMe Pay: The innovation built on top of China's payment technology

The timing was also good. From 2014 to 2018, the number of inbound tourists in Japan doubled every year. Chinese tourists were the largest by country. Chinese tourists also spend more per person. Twenty-five per cent of all inbound were Chinese in numbers. However, their spending was forty per cent among all inbound tourists.

Chinese tourists bought luxurious goods, cosmetics and electronic products and they spent more money on meals. Since we also had a payment service at the storefront to enable payment of WeChat Pay and Alipay, which Chinese people use, more and more merchants in retail, hotel, taxi and travel industries started to ask for our payment products. Seeing the demand for QR-code payment services, we separated our payment service from Japan Foodie and gave it a new name, TakeMe Pay. The meaning was, take me to anywhere, do anything and pay conveniently. The concept was to have the merchant use one QR code to accept payment from all different kinds of eWallets in the world.

It was like the Square for eWallets. QR-code payment started in China, other Asian countries followed and many eWallet companies copied the success. However, each country had many different QR-code-based eWallets. Each eWallet used a different QR code. Those QR codes were not compatible with each other. There were countries that tried to standardise it, such as Singapore. However, there was no global standard for QR code payment. Therefore, if the merchant wanted to accept eWallets from different countries, it had to have multiple QR codes at the shopfront, which is not convenient.

TakeMe Pay became a breakthrough again because we integrated all QR codes into one. Also, at the backend, contracting and payout were also combined into one process.

TakeMe Pay's pricing was also cheaper than other payment methods. As a result, the number of merchants grew from three hundred to three thousand in 2018 and to fifty-five thousand in 2019.

The people problem

The business went well. However, I started to have people problems.

The other two co-founders left the company one year into the operation. They couldn't leave their current companies and join me on a full-time basis. I also felt their contribution to the company was limited. I bought back some of their shares and kept a good relationship with them.

In the middle of the high growth and fundraising, suddenly the CTO quit without giving me a clear reason. I was frustrated because I felt I never fully understood him. There had always been a distance between us. I had never had a heart-to-heart conversation with him. What's worst was the entire engineering team left with him. I talked to each one of the five engineers. They gave me some vague reasons that I didn't think were convincing. I even told the CTO that it was irresponsible to quit at the crucial timing of fundraising and asked him to stay for a few more months until we got the funds. After many long meetings with him, he still didn't give me a clear reason and insisted on quitting.

Money is not a problem anymore!

In May 2018, I met Mr. H, a consultant who advised wealthy business owners on succession plans. Mr. H was amazed by my background and my business and told me, "You are going to be the next Jeff Bezos or Jack Ma." When I told him I was raising series A and it was painstaking to raise funds while managing my company, he asked: "How much money do you want?" "One billion yen," I answered. "OK. Come and speak at my seminar next week." He offered me the opportunity to give his clients a thirty-minute presentation at his monthly seminar. He had been doing consulting for over thirty years and had written fourteen books. He had accumulated about three hundred clients. The net worth of his clients ranged from three to thirty billion yen.

On the day of the seminar, there were about fifty people in a large conference room. Mr. H introduced me to his clients with my background in Goldman Sachs, Stanford GSB, venture capital and starting two companies in China. He told them I was the rising star in Japan's entrepreneur world. My business was going to be the next Amazon or Alibaba.

I delivered my presentation to the investors as usual, which I had done hundreds of times. After that, he said to his clients: "TakeMe is raising a round now. Today, Mr. Dong is giving you a special opportunity to invest twenty million yen per person. I know you may want to invest more. However, since this is a limited opportunity, he can only take twenty million yen per person. Please sign up with me within today." He had me remain standing on the stage and his clients lined up to shake hands with me. I felt I was like a star.

After that, I joined their dinner with them. There were eight round tables in a large banquet hall. I moved from table to table to greet everyone. I kept talking to people and barely had time to eat.

The next morning, I went to see Mr. H in his office. Mr. H said: "You did really well last night. You were a star. Guess how much money we raised? Eight hundred and forty million!" I was shocked and amazed. "See how easy it is for me to raise money for you? This is only the beginning. I am your producer now." He smiled at me triumphantly and continued, "From now on, you can forget about fundraising and focus on building the next Amazon. Problems can be solved and money is not your problem anymore."

"What's your biggest bottleneck between now and IPO?" he asked. "People?" I thought for a second and replied: "In order to go IPO, I need a team that has the experience or calibre to take the company IPO. My current team is not good enough." "Can we solve the people problem with money?" I asked him. "Yes. We can hire the best head-hunters to bring you the top talents and pay them more than your competitors," he answered.

It felt like a dream come true! "Wow! Money is not a problem anymore!" I felt I could do anything.

Building the Dream Team

With eight hundred and forty million yen committed, other institutional investors joined the round as well. We closed Series A financing with one billion yen.

Again, I tasted success. I was featured by Forbes and among the list of "twenty rising stars in Japan" and "two hundred most successful entrepreneurs in Japan". I got invitations to speak at various events and seminars. Reporters kept chasing me for interviews.

I started building the company as a public company. First, I found an office space in one of the most prestigious office buildings in Tokyo, the New Kasumigaseki Building. It was on the eighteenth floor, with five hundred square metres to hold one hundred and fifty people in the next three years. At that time, we only had seventeen people. The moment I walked into the empty office space; I was amazed by the view. I could overlook the parliament house, the residence of the Prime Minister and the Emperor's Palace. I felt I was on top of Japan. I decided immediately because I was thinking we need an office like this for the image of a public company. I was imagining myself and the executive team members sitting in the office and discussing business with our business partners, bankers and lawyers.

I started hiring the top management team. I had a typical problem that start-ups usually have. At the beginning of the company, I didn't have money to hire expensive talents. The people I hired were juniors. Even when we expanded to seventeen people, there was still a lack of middle management. I felt the bottleneck of managing too many junior people. Not only did I have twelve reporting lines, but I also needed to give detailed instructions for each of them because they had little experience. I felt my team didn't understand what I was talking about. The team members' feedback was that my instructions were vague and constantly changing. However, I didn't feel that way. I thought my strategy was clear and my goals were always the same. There was a disconnect between me and the team.

One of the angel investors told me that was natural. "Your capability and vision are way beyond your junior teammates. Of course, they don't understand you. Don't even expect them to understand. Just tell them what to do." He was a successful entrepreneur who built his business in eight years and sold it for twenty million dollars. He offered to speak to our team members at our monthly meeting. He stood in front of all the team members and talked about his stories of building and selling his company. "I invested in Lu because I knew he was better than me. He could build a much bigger company than me." He said: "Remember, Lu is always right. Just listen to him and do what he tells you to do."

I felt I was like a small king. Finally, someone understood me and spoke for me.

I drew an organisational chart with many blank boxes to hire. I gathered many head-hunters and recruiters and gave them those positions to fill. Within a busy process of interviewing, I hired eight top management team members in three months.

The COO used to be a founder and CEO of a public company in Japan. He sold the company after the IPO and lived a semi-retired life. I convinced him to join us and to "do it again". The CFO used to be my peer at Goldman Sachs. He worked at a Japanese security firm for fifteen years as a manager in sales, trading convertible bonds. The CTO used to work at big Chinese technology companies as a product manager. He had thirty thousand followers on Twitter and was somehow famous among engineers in China. The VP of payment used to be a CEO of a payment gateway company in Japan. The Head of Sales, Mr. T, was introduced by a friend to be the star of sales in a PR company. He used to be a professional wrestler who attended the Beijing Olympics. The head of Southeast Asia used to be my friend back in Beijing. He was a third-generation Chinese who grew up in Indonesia. After spending twenty years in China and the US, he had just moved back to Jakarta. The head of strategy was an ex BCG guy who used to be a semi-pro soccer player. The head of the Taiwan office used to be an entrepreneur who sold his travel company to a big company.

It was amazing that we could hire such a stellar management team within three months. The Management Team page of my investor pitch deck looked like this was the team that could ring the bell at the Tokyo Stock Exchange.

We arranged a trip with all the top executive management to Beijing. I showed them the most advanced business models and technologies in retail, restaurant and payment. I had the team experience the services themselves as customers. We went shopping at Hema supermarket to experience the new retail technology of online–merges–offline.

We went to the famous restaurant Haidilao to experience how robotic and entertainment merged with dining. We went to the Xiaomi store to see how Xiaomi combined an Apple store with Muji and created a new category. We went to sing karaoke and experienced how everything was done on a smartphone instead of a big machine. We rode MoBike on the street by scanning a QR code. I showed them how advanced some areas of China were and showed them the future of Japan.

We spent a whole day in our Beijing office. I proposed our vision, mission, value and strategy. The whole team was fired up to build a unicorn that could change Japan.

The people problems became crisis

We went back to Japan. I thought everything should be carried out according to the plan. However, after a few months, I found the performance of the team didn't meet my expectation. The team became bigger and bigger. There were meetings after meetings.

However, we couldn't meet the sales KPIs. I started to put more pressure on the Head of Sales, Mr. T. However, he always gave me excuses. One day, at a management meeting, I became angry when I heard his excuses: "Shut up and stop giving me excuses!" I shouted and pointed my finger at him. He shut up, looked around and shrugged.

From that moment, his attitude changed and became more sarcastic. He started challenging me in front of the public with a sneer on his face. I thought I hired the wrong person and thought of ways to fire him.

The position of Head of Sales had always been my biggest problem. Within the first three years, there had been eight Heads of Sales. They were always over-promising and under-delivering. None of them could achieve the growth target and maintain a good culture at the same time. The morale of the sales team was bad. The turnover of the sales team was high.

One day, we got a letter from a law firm and found out that our previous CTO and three employees had sued us for not granting them the stock options. I was furious that they not only left irresponsibly but also sued us for stock options they weren't entitled to.

Furthermore, at the management meeting, the Sales Head, Mr. T, asked me about this lawsuit and asked for a solution: "I heard you are doing another round of fundraising. I doubt any investor would invest in a start-up that has a lawsuit. If we don't close the next round, we will run out of money and go bankrupt!" He talked loudly. I sensed he was trying to make a big deal. He even seemed excited while talking. I was irritated and told him: "The lawsuit and fundraising are on a need-to-know basis and you don't need to know." However, after the meeting, he walked out to the office floor and told everyone about the lawsuit. I knew he wanted to irritate me and have me fire him. Then he could get a severance package from the company. I didn't do that but, instead, put more pressure on his sales target. I was preparing a war with him.

The conflict between me and the Head of Sales became more and more obvious. With worries and deteriorating morale among team members, not only employees but also management team members started to resign. The COO resigned within six months. The VP of Payment and the Head of Strategy also resigned.

The Conspiracy

However, to my surprise, within a month, Mr. T sent me an email and resigned. I thought, "Great that made my life easier." He handed back the computer to the CFO. At that time, our CFO oversaw Finance, Legal, HR and Administration. I trusted him because he had been one of my best friends for the past twenty years.

The next day, the CFO pulled me to the conference room, closed the door and whispered: "Take a look at this." "Why whisper?" I asked him. He pointed his finger to the ceiling and hinted that people outside could hear us because the walls were not sealed with the ceiling. I was shocked when I looked at the computer screen.

Apparently, when Mr. T returned his computer to the company, he forgot to log out of his social media accounts, such as Facebook Messenger and LINE. Not only could we see his chat history, but we could also see his ongoing chats while he was logged in from other devices. The CFO told me he spent the whole night going through Mr. T's chats with previous employees and found out he staged the lawsuit and was hoping to get a settlement of one hundred million yen from the company. As I went through the chats, I felt I discovered a huge underground world. I got the complete picture.

First, our ex-CTO resigned, took the entire engineering team and started his own company by copying our payment technology. He also sabotaged our server so that there were always problems in the database. Right after Mr. T came back from our trip to Beijing, he already felt the conflict with me. However, instead of telling me, he reached out to the ex-CTO and other ex-employees who were resentful of me. They even created a monthly gathering to strategise the attacks against me. They gave me a nickname, Stupid Dong. They even got the ex-accounting person to steal our financials and tried to figure out how much money the company had in the banks.

Everything was clearly written in the chat. Apparently, their strategy was to have the ex-CTO and other ex-employees sue the company. They betted since I needed to raise funding for the existence of the company, I would settle with them by paying one hundred million yen and get rid of the lawsuit as soon as I could so that I could continue fundraising. After his resignation, Mr. T reached out to our employees to persuade them to leave the company by spreading rumours that the company was going bankrupt. Furthermore, Mr. T even went to meet with several of our shareholders, including Mr. H, to spread the rumour and told them that I stole money from the company and bought luxurious cars for myself.

What evil people they were! I was furious about Mr. T, the ex-CTO and the other ex-employees. "Why did they all gang up against us?" I couldn't understand. I felt terrible imagining Mr. T writing those chats and staging the conspiracy sitting at his desk in our office while getting paid by us for months. No wonder he had that sneer on his face! "They are thieves, criminals and terrorists!" I thought. I needed to retaliate and destroy them.

However, after revealing the materials to our lawyer, he advised us to settle the lawsuit with our ex-employees and not create a war against Mr. T. After all, we still wanted to raise funds from institutional investors and go IPO. We didn't want to cause potential further damage and risk our company's future. We wanted to get rid of the lawsuit as soon as possible.

Brute-force the IPO

I understood the situation. "The best defence is the offence," I thought. I agreed to negotiate with them and settle for the lowest amount. At the same time, not only did I continue fundraising, but I also decided to start the IPO filing process. "Nobody could stop me!" I told myself. I wanted to use the IPO process to give both the team members and shareholders hope and confidence.

The IPO preparation itself was a huge project. We put together a four-people team to focus on the IPO process. The prerequisite for applying to the Tokyo Stock Exchange was to have two years of auditing by a reputable accounting firm and sponsorship by an investment bank. We managed to find connections and paid a consultant to finally get a second-tier audit firm to agree to do a Short Review. It was a one hundred and eighty-question checklist about the current status of the company.

The Short Review started in October 2019 and was projected to finish by the end of December. The goal was to start the official IPO audit on 1 April, 2020, when our new fiscal year began.

Better Company project by Ikemoto-san, the COO

In August 2019, Ikemoto-san joined our company as the COO. I chased him for ten months to join us. He had a great track record of co-founding and selling his business, Spotlight, a location-based CRM start-up, to Rakuten. He then became the CEO of the company after the acquisition. He spent another four years turning the company profitable. When he made himself available on the job market, more than twenty companies offered him positions from COO to CEO. However, he took his time to get to know each of the companies. We met every month for many hours to talk about our backgrounds, dreams and the challenges I was facing. We got to know each other more and more.

Since he also had experience as an HR consultant, he suggested doing a three-month consulting project with us because I faced many management problems. We both agreed with the project; Ikemoto-san not only would understand the inside-out of the company by interviewing every person in the company, but he would also recommend solutions to solve the problems. He could make a decision after the project. I decided to honestly show him everything about the company.

We met once per month to go through his findings and agreed on the next steps. To my surprise, after interviewing everyone in the company, Ikemoto-san's reaction was generally positive. He said that although there were some complaints from the employees, most of the employees were pure and had faith in the company. He believed those problems could be fixed.

My final push was to send him to Beijing to experience the new online-merges-offline economy I was talking about. Ikemoto-san grew up in Japan and had never studied or worked overseas. I had our general manager in Beijing show him all the new retail and restaurant technology companies, like we did last time.

On the final day of his three-day trip, he called me from Beijing. "I have decided to join TakeMe!" he said. I was so happy. I almost felt like when a girl I had been dating and chasing for ten months finally agreed to marry me.

At the welcome dinner, when he came back to Japan, he told me the reasons why he decided to join me. He said he liked the vision and people of TakeMe. He felt he could not only challenge himself in an international environment, but he could also both contribute to the business and solve the management problems. When I asked him about his motivation, he said that what gave him the most joy was seeing his subordinates grow and succeed.

Right after Ikemoto-san joined the company, he started a project called Better Company by putting together a small project team across the company. The team members were selected based on their interviews. They were the core team members. Ikemoto-san said those were the people who had faith in the company and had ideas to make the changes.

After work, they met once a week in a separate office to work on the Better Company project. Nobody outside the project team, including me, knew what they were doing.

I was invited to their final presentation after a month. The format of the presentation was that every team member took turns to present. In the first half, they talked about the problems in the company. In the second half, they proposed a set of new values for the company, ReLOVE. The three values for the company, Love, Trust and Excellence, were created by me. Their proposal of new values was Respect, Logical, Ownership, Velocity and Exceptional.

When each of them went to present, I saw the young team members spoke with passion and excitement. Their eyes and faces were shining. I felt they were my children and saying: "Daddy, we misunderstood you before. We now know your good intention for us. From now on, you don't have to bear the burden by yourself. You have us. Let's do it together!" I was deeply touched and cried. We all hugged and cried together. I was amazed at how much change Ikemoto-san made in people within one month.

Learnings from Ikemoto-san

Ikemoto-san also handled the negotiation and settlement of the lawsuit. After he reviewed the historical chat by Mr. T, he said: "There must be something that Mr. T wasn't content with." Nattoku was the Japanese word he always used. It means understanding and consent. I was surprised to see how calm he was when he spoke. He wasn't emotional at all, unlike the CFO and me. He didn't immediately say they were criminals or terrorists. He repeated a couple of times: "There must be something that happened to them that they didn't understand or didn't agree with."

This was my biggest learning from Ikemoto-san. His principle for dealing with people, whether they are employees, clients, or shareholders, had always been Nattoku, meaning gaining full understanding and consent. Compared to him, I often forced people to do things without gaining their full understanding and consent.

At first, I felt his way was too slow. I was quick on judging people. I used to be proud of judging a new employee's capability after one month. I thought I was patient enough to give that person feedback and observe for another month. Then if there was no change, I would let go of that person after the third month. I believed that people didn't change. If it was not a right fit, why bother wasting time on each other?

After Ikemoto-san joined, he also identified a couple of employees who should be let go. However, Ikemoto-san spent month after month communicating with them. To me, I thought it was wasting shareholders' money and our time. We had already made decisions to let go of them. Why spend the extra money and so much time with them?

However, I started to realise that he was right. Because of the extra time and number of meetings with the employees, they fully consented to the decision. Also, they found new jobs during that time. We held farewell parties for them. They left with smiles on their faces.

Ikemoto-san truly respected our employees by gaining their understanding and consent. He gave them time to think and prepare. The employees left without bad feelings about the company. However, my handling of the firing process would make them feel disrespected. They didn't tell me the truth about why they left. They left and became enemies of the company. They sought chances for revenge. Furthermore, the current employees were watching the whole situation. They might think this could happen to them, too, some day. I said the company values were love and trust. However, I didn't treat them with love and trust. I didn't walk my talk. No wonder they called me a dictator and a hypocrite. After my reflection, I decided to learn from Ikemoto-san's way of treating people and gave him the responsibility to manage people.

There was much good news In December 2019. We had our best sales ever. We completed our Short Review with the audit firm. The result was good. They agreed to enter the IPO audit from the beginning of our next fiscal year,

April 2020. The fundraising for Series B went well. We soft-circled ninety per cent of the one-billion-yen round. Most of the due diligence was done. We were working with lawyers on closing documents toward the closing date, the end of March 2020. Not only were the Japanese investors interested in us, but a few overseas investors were committed to investing in us as well. Our valuation was fourteen billion yen. The morale of the team members was high with the leadership of Ikemoto-san.

Devastated by Covid

However, Covid19 started to break out in China in January 2020. Our revenue kept dropping every month, with fewer and fewer international tourists travelling to Japan. By March, international travel was completely stopped. Our revenue from foreign tourist reservations for restaurants became zero. Our payment revenue dropped to half because of restrictions on dining in restaurants in Japan.

We lost ninety per cent of our revenue within four months. We couldn't close the series B financing because the committed investors pulled out. The foreign investors apologised to us and said they had to stop investing because not only had their share prices dropped by fifty per cent, but they also had to lay off people internally.

Not only did we have to stop our IPO process, but we also had to face the situation that we only had two months of cash runway.

We had to cut down costs to the minimum to survive. At the same time, I asked all existing shareholders to support us by investing more.

Ikemoto-san and I agreed to cut our salaries to zero. Managers cut to half and the employees cut thirty per cent of their salaries. However, that was not enough. We had no choice but to reduce our staff from forty-six to twenty. We moved our big office, which was prepared to hold one hundred and fifty people, into a shared office with one twenty-square-metre room that fit ten people. We figured we would just have team members rotate and come to the office if needed. This reduced our rent by eighty per cent.

The hardest time was letting go of twenty-six team members over Zoom. I made a speech to all the team members: "Imagine I was an athlete aiming for a gold medal at the Olympic games. Suddenly, I lost my legs in an accident. I had to let go of my legs. It's not my legs' fault. However, I have no choice. You are my legs. It's painful to lose you." I was tearing up when I said it. "However," I continued, "We still have hope. We don't give up. Even without legs, we are still going to aim for a gold medal at the Special Olympics!"

We granted all the team members who left the company fifty per cent of the stock options they owned. That was an exception. Normally in Japan's start-ups, when employees leave the company, all of their stock options would be expired.

My Depression

Those two months were like dark winters. Every day, I was locked at home and worked hard. I had one-on-one Zoom calls with leaving team members. I was calling each of our shareholders. I called many VCs and banks. At the same time, I worked with existing team members to restructure the operation and tried to find ways to create revenues. I worked with the finance team to go through each line of our P/L to seek costs to cut. I had to create many versions of financial projections with different scenarios, including the worst-case one. It was depressing. I had to smile and be confident in front of the camera. After a long day of work, I was exhausted. I couldn't eat. I couldn't sleep at night. I couldn't stop thinking about the consequences. The only way I could release my stress was through alcohol.

At first, I was drinking wine at night to put myself to sleep. The sleepless nights were long. Then I started drinking in the afternoon. Then I started to drink during the day. I started to drink one bottle of wine per day. Then I started to finish two bottles. Then I felt the wine was too weak and started to drink whiskey. It's cheaper and stronger. On the weekends, I even started drinking in the morning.

My wife silently watched me and supported me by cooking every day and taking care of our daughter. I hated to watch the TV because it was all about Covid. I spent most of the time in my room in front of my computer.

One night at the dinner table, my wife prepared dinner and called me to have dinner with the family. I had already finished one bottle of wine and was drinking whiskey and I was drunk. Somehow, I got irritated and angry with her. I stood up and went to the kitchen. I grabbed a knife and handed it to her. "You hate me right; just kill me!" I shouted at her. My wife and daughter were frightened and froze for a few seconds. "OK, if you don't do it, I am gonna do it myself." I continued shouting and started pointing the knife at myself. My daughter was scared and started crying.

Suddenly, I felt like I was watching myself from Heaven. "What am I doing?" I woke up and realised what I was doing. My wife took our daughter to the bedroom and closed the door.

I regretted my stupid behaviour and reflected. I was supposed to make my family happy and protect them. As a husband and father, I am supposed to give them safety and security. However, instead, I became their threat. I felt deeply ashamed of myself. I realised I was wrong. I was trying to avoid facing the reality. I was thinking and acting like a victim.

My turning point: search for the wisdom

I decided to change. However, I knew I couldn't do this by myself. I reached out to Ory, one of my best friends whom I had brought into my company and who was based in Jakarta. I remembered he was a Christian. At that moment, the only thing I could rely on was God. He prayed for me. We prayed together for God to save us.

The next morning, we started to read the Bible and pray. We wanted to get wisdom from God just like Solomon did. Solomon asked for wisdom and God gave him everything. We have continued from that day until today – more three years. This completely changed my life. We decided we would continue to do this until the last day of our lives.

Ory introduced a book for me to read, 'Business By The Book'. It was written in the 80s by Larry Burkett, the founder of Crown Financial Ministries. The book introduced the concept of applying Biblical principles to running businesses.

I also took a training course by another Christian brother, Carl Thong, whose content was largely based on Ken Blanchard's Servant Leadership theory. It was an eye-opening experience.

Business By The Book and my self-reflection

I had been a Christian for twelve years, but I had always been an "underground Christian". I tried to be a good person so that I could go to Heaven when facing judgment day. However, I had never tried to use the Bible as a guide to run my businesses. All my business training was from Goldman Sachs and Stanford GSB. I always thought that American-style business skills were the best in the world. However, after reading 'Business By The Book' and taking the training course of Servant Leadership, many of my fundamental values and views about business completely changed. I started to realise that it was me who caused many problems in the company. The scarier discovery was that I kept repeating the same mistakes.

I started to learn about my true self. I always felt the calling of making a difference in people's lives. I had the strength of business skills and actions to quickly turn ideas into businesses. I always focused on the pain points of customers and was good at designing products to solve problems. I was passionate, resilient and perseverant. That was why I could identify opportunities and start businesses quickly, going from zero to one.

However, I had a fundamentally flawed mindset. I was using people to achieve my goals as a leader. Over time, I developed a sense of entitlement to being a CEO. My mindset was that my employees serve me instead of I serve them. My attitude and behaviour were reflecting my mindset. I said love and trust were our values; however, I didn't really love and trust my teammates. My purpose in hiring them was to fulfill my purpose of success – not necessarily for their success. No wonder why some ex-employees thought I was a dictator and hypocrite. They must have thought I was selfish. I was the one who was destroying our culture.

Another mistake I made was relying on money to solve problems. I realised that not only could money not solve people problems, but money also couldn't solve most problems. Conversely, money could create problems. If I used the money to hire people by increasing their salaries and giving them hope to make more money after the IPO, I could only hire people who love money instead of loving our vision, mission, values, products and customers.

Because of my background, it was easier for me to raise money than to make money. I had changed from customer-focused to investor-focused when the company had initial success and got large funding from investors. My goals had shifted from the continued improvement of products and services that would ultimately benefit customers to the IPO and valuation of the company.

The start of change

After seeing my blindness to my flawed mindset, I became very careful saying anything or making any decisions. I realised my initial reactions could be wrong. I took time to think whether my heart was right by asking myself: "What would Jesus do if He was in my situation? Is my intention serving myself or others? Is this fit the best interest of others? Do they fully understand and consent?"

One day, Ikemoto-san and I agreed to give some critical feedback to a manager who oversaw fundraising because he didn't meet his target. We prepared for his leaving as the worst-case scenario. My usual way of communication would be: "Your performance didn't meet the target that you promised to the company. Therefore, we are giving you a verbal warning and going to reduce your salary". I prayed before the meeting that I would be a servant leader and love him. When the meeting started, I said: "I am sorry to hear that your performance was lower than you expected. It's my fault. As a leader, my job is to support you so that you can be the best of yourself. You performed well in your previous company. However, you didn't perform well here. It's my responsibility." Seeing his surprised face, I was surprised as well about my own words. They came out naturally and genuinely from my heart. He paused for a few seconds and responded: "No, no, no, it's my fault. I could have done better." "What's the biggest barrier that prevents you from achieving your goals? How can I help you?" I looked him in the eye and asked. Clearly, he wasn't prepared for this kind of conversation. I felt he was preparing an argument and a fight over the deduction of his salary. I gave him time to think and offered to talk at any time. However, after two weeks, he resigned. There was no fight or argument. I felt sorry for his leaving and told him it was a loss for both him and the company.

Rescue of the company and myself

In order to rescue the company, Fukuhara-san held a meeting with his employees and his friends in the restaurant business. I gave a presentation about our business and our current situation. Fukuhara-san asked everybody to invest and help us survive. Store managers and even previous employees of Fukumimi all made the investment from their savings. Some put in ten thousand dollars, some put in one thousand dollars and some put in fifteen thousand dollars. I was deeply touched by their generosity and faith in us. They were in the restaurant business, which was badly damaged by Covid as well. They didn't know when it would be over, but they used their savings to rescue us.

Other shareholders heard about this and were touched as well. Together, our existing shareholders put together one hundred and sixty million yen to rescue the company.

Other than equity, I was running around asking banks to loan us money as well. However, since we had no assets for collateral, most of the banks rejected us.

I visited Japan Finance Corporate, a semi-government bank. I prepared for another rejection. To my surprise, the manager said to me: "Your company had been helping the restaurants in Japan to increase their revenue and improve the customer experience of foreign tourists. You had a healthy business model. We can't let you go bankrupt because of Covid." They offered to lend us five hundred million yen with very low interest to be paid after two years. I almost broke into tears. I thanked them for rescuing our company and promised them we would continue to help restaurants in Japan to survive and thrive.

With rescue funding from shareholders, friends and the bank, we survived for two years during Covid. Our team became much smaller but much stronger. Everyone had the mentality to try their best to make money to help the company survive. In the monthly town hall meeting, I told the team the good news about getting the funding. At the same time, I told the team that I was wrong by aiming for the gold medal of the Special Olympics. It was a compromise. It was a victim mentality. Instead, we should still try to win a gold medal in a different game in the Olympic games. We should always focus on our strengths and try to be the winner no matter what happens. I shared my experience of a suicide attempt, learning from the Bible and going through servant leadership training. I said: "TakeMe is ours, not mine. Let's use this opportunity to learn and practice love. To love each other and to love our clients means to make a difference in their lives so that they can be the best of themselves. I need to learn from you and practice with you. Please don't listen to what I say; watch what I do."

I could see the people nodding their heads. Some even broke into tears. Some teammates came to me and shook my hand and told me it was the best speech I made.

The experience of surviving Covid gave me so many lessons and completely changed my life. It was a painful but transforming experience, turning me from a person who selfishly pursued personal success by using people to a servant leader who focuses on others' success.

Today, I feel I am still a beginner. I am still learning to be a good servant leader. I am still learning to apply Biblical principles to various situations in business and with people. I still discover my blindness on a daily basis. It keeps me humble. I feel I have no pride and no fear at the same time. I have no pride in myself because I am a sinner. I have no fear because I know as long as I keep walking on the narrow path to His Kingdom, I have His covenant that I will serve Him in His Kingdom forever.

LU DONG

About the Author

Lu Dong is the founder and CEO of TakeMe Co, Ltd. and he is a third-time entrepreneur. He was born in Beijing, China. In 1989, Lu survived the Tiananmen massacre and moved to Japan at the age of twenty. Knowing no one and speaking no Japanese, Lu survived by washing dishes at night in a restaurant and going to language school during the day. Lu got into college and studied economics and computer science. After graduation, Lu worked at Goldman Sachs. Lu earned an MBA at Stanford.

Lu was inspired at Stanford to be an entrepreneur. After graduation, he went back to China and started two e-commerce companies. During that time, Lu started believing in Jesus and attending small groups in underground churches in Beijing. After spending ten years in China, Lu sold the businesses and returned to Japan.

In 2016, Lu started his third company, TakeMe, applying what he learned in China to Japan. TakeMe generates revenues for local restaurants through online reservations for international tourists. TakeMe also provides digital order and QR payment solutions for merchants. The goal is to help small businesses not only to survive but also thrive during the digital transformation.

Covid19 almost destroyed TakeMe. However, Lu thanks God for using Covid to bring him closer to Him. He started to rely on God only and walk the servant leadership path. Lu's mission is to use his business to glorify God by making a difference in others' lives.

Lu lives in Tokyo with his wife Hideko and daughter Ai. Hideko is a professional flamenco dancer and teacher in Japan. The family enjoys traveling in Japan and other countries.

About PublishU

PublishU is transforming the world of publishing.

PublishU has developed a new and unique approach to publishing books, offering a three-step guided journey to becoming a globally published author!

We enable hundreds of people a year to write their book within 100-days, publish their book in 100-days and launch their book over 100-days to impact tens of thousands of people worldwide.

The journey is transformative, one author said,

"I never thought I would be able to write a book, let alone in 100 days... now I'm asking myself what else have I told myself that can't be done that actually can?'"

To find out more visit
www.PublishU.com

LU DONG

Made in the USA
Columbia, SC
13 June 2024